Negotiating

PHILIP O'CONNOR, ADRIAN PILBEAM
AND FIONA SCOTT-BARRETT

Longman

SERIES EDITOR NINA O'DRISCOLL
WITH MARK ELLIS AND ADRIAN PILBEAM

The authors work for Language Training Services

Addison Wesley Longman Limited
Edinburgh Gate, Harlow,
Essex CM20 2JE, England
and Associated Companies throughout the world.

First published 1992
Sixth impression 1998

Designed and set by Design Locker in
Monotype PostScript Gill Sans 10 on 12pt

Printed in China
SWTC/06

ISBN 0 582 06443 0

Acknowledgements

We are grateful to the following for their permission to reproduce
copyright material:

Delta Airlines for page 50. Lufthansa German Airlines for page 49.
Sietar International (The Society for Intercultural Education,
Training and Research) 733 15th St, NW, Suite 900, Washington DC
20005, USA for page 86.

Cartoons by Bill Caldwell and Sax.

Cover photograph by The Telegraph Colour Library.

Contents

Unit 5: Options

Unit 6: Bidding

Unit 7: Bargaining

Unit 8: Settling and concluding

Introduction to the learner

Negotiating is part of the *Longman Business English Skills* series. It presents and practises language to help you be more effective when negotiating internationally. It is suitable for business and professional people who already have a good working knowledge of English.

Objectives

The aim of this material is to:
- develop awareness of the different stages of a negotiation
- present the language appropriate to each stage
- give practice in listening to and using this language in controlled situations
- develop awareness of cultural differences in negotiating styles

The model of negotiation

There are different approaches to negotiating. These are determined, to a large extent, by the situation; for example, you will approach a one-off situation, such as buying or selling a house in a different way to negotiating a joint-venture agreement which will lead to a long-term relationship between two or more companies.

The model of negotiating presented in this book is in the context of building a potentially long-term business relationship. It is based particularly on the research of the Harvard Negotiation Project which suggests that in most negotiating situations it is possible to 'pursue your own interests while maintaining good human relations with [people] whose interests conflict with yours'.[1] The emphasis throughout this book, therefore, is on a collaborative rather than a confrontational approach.

For the purposes of this book, the members of your own negotiating team are defined as your 'negotiating partners' and the people in the other team are referred to as 'the other side' or 'the other party'.

The model of English

The language presented in this book shows how to work with this collaborative model of negotiation in English. For this reason, language associated with confrontational tactics such as 'attacking' or 'threatening' is not included but, where appropriate, language for dealing with a confrontational approach is included.

As English is frequently the medium of international negotiations, the language presented in this book is accurate and appropriate 'international English', not specifically 'British' or 'American English'.

The material

The material is designed for you to use on your own, or with a teacher. It consists of an audio-cassette with a book. The book and the cassette should be used together.

The cassette contains extracts from negotiations which provide a model of language, and some of the practice tasks. All material on the cassette is marked 📼 in the book.

There are eight units. Each unit covers a different stage of a collaborative negotiation, beginning with relationship building and ending with settling and concluding. With the exception of Unit 8, which is a short unit, each unit has the following sections:

A Language

This section presents and practises language used by one person at a time, for example, to introduce an idea, to put forward an option, to introduce objectives.

B Interaction

This section presents and practises language for reacting to what other people have said, for example, for responding to questions, for correcting misunderstandings, for accepting or rejecting proposals.

C Style

This section looks at different ways of getting your point across, depending on the effect you want to create. It shows that you always have a choice, for example, between direct or indirect language, and that some choices are more appropriate than others within the context of a collaborative negotiation.

D Cross-cultural differences

People from different cultures may have different approaches to negotiating. This section presents some examples of different approaches and some of the reasons for them. Of course, not every person from that culture will behave in that way.

Using the material

Sections A, B and C have the following steps:

Focus

There are two parts to this step. In sections A and B, you listen to part of a negotiation which is recorded on the cassette and answer some general questions to check your understanding. Then you listen to the same recording again and, while you are listening, you fill in the missing words. You may need to stop the cassette and play some extracts several times. The purpose of the Focus step in sections A and B is to present language which will be useful to you in the practice tasks, and when you take part in 'real-life' negotiations.

In section C, the format of the Focus step varies from unit to unit. The purpose of this step is to raise your awareness of the effects of choosing different ways to make the same point.

Summary

This gives you a summary of useful language and interaction techniques. You should refer to this before you do the practice tasks for each section. It is also designed as reference material for when you are preparing for a negotiation in English.

Tasks

These practise the language and interaction points from the summaries. Some of the tasks are on cassette. These are indicated by the symbol 🖭 in your book. You may want to record yourself doing some of the tasks so that you can compare your version with the model version. These tasks are indicated by the symbol 🖭 🔊 in your book.

Section D has the following steps:

Focus

In this step, different approaches to negotiating are presented in the form of a short quiz or case-study. If working in a group, or with a teacher, you may want to use these activities as a basis for discussion.

Summary

This includes comments on important underlying cultural differences, based on the research work of several experts in cross-cultural communication.

The key

After each unit there is a key. This contains the tapescripts for all the recorded materials in the unit, and suggested answers to the tasks. In many tasks there are several possible 'right' answers or versions, and only one or two are given in the key. The model version in the key is only a suggestion. If your version is different, it will not be wrong as long as it has a similar style and form to the model version.

---

[1] Reference to *Getting to Yes, Negotiating Agreement without Giving in*, Fisher and Ury, Arrow Books (1981)

Relationship building

A Language	How to greet and introduce people
B Interaction	How to keep a conversation moving
C Style	What to call people
D Cross-cultural differences	What would you do?

Background

Two representatives of British Inland, a British domestic airline, are visiting Brazil to have a meeting with representatives of AMB (Aircraft Manufacturers of Brazil). The purpose of the visit is to hold preliminary negotiations about the possible purchase of aircraft from AMB.

A Language – How to greet and introduce people

A1 Focus

First impressions can be important. Therefore, when you meet the other side before the negotiation begins, you should try to establish a good atmosphere. This relationship building stage can often set the climate for the whole negotiation.

 Listen to tape A1. You will now hear a conversation which takes place at the visitors' hotel in São Paulo. One of the Brazilians from AMB comes to meet them in the hotel lobby.

Taking part in the conversation are

John Crow	General Manager, British Inland
Peter Burnell	Purchasing Manager, British Inland
Osorio da Silva	Technical Sales Manager, AMB
Paulo Santos	Head of Overseas Sales Division, AMB

1. Decide if the following statements are *true* or *false*.
   a. Osorio da Silva has met both of the British people before.
   b. The visitors suggest having a drink before dinner.
   c. Paulo Santos has met John Crow before.
   d. Paulo Santos has met Peter Burnell before.

   Check your answers in the key **A1.1**

2. Listen to tape A1 again and complete the missing words in the extracts. Then read the notes on the right.

	Extract 1	*Notes*
OSORIO DA SILVA	Excuse me. .... Mr Crow and Mr Burnell from British Inland?	*Checks the visitors' identity*
JOHN CROW	That's right. .... John Crow,	*Identifies himself and his colleague*
	and .... Peter Burnell.	
OSORIO DA SILVA	.... ?	*Greets them*
	.... Osorio da Silva.	*Identifies himself and gives details of his job*
	.... the .... at AMB.	

	Extract 2	
PAULO SANTOS	.... , it's	*Greets John Crow*
	.... How .... ?	
JOHN CROW	.... , Paulo. .... , ...	*Greets Paulo Santos*
	It's .... in Brazil.	*Adds a favourable comment*

	Extract 3	
JOHN CROW	....	*Introduces Peter Burnell*
	.... , Peter Burnell.	
	.... new	*Gives details of his job*
	Peter, ... Paulo Santos, ...	*Introduces Paulo Santos and gives details of his job*
	.... AMB's Overseas Sales Division.	
PAULO SANTOS	....	*Greets Peter Burnell*
	.... , Mr Burnell.	
PETER BURNELL	....	*Replies*
	.... , too.	

Check your answers in the key **A1.2**

A2 Language summary

At first meetings it is helpful to:
- identify yourself and other people clearly by name.
- add any other relevant details about your or their job or company.

Checking other people's identities

> **Excuse me. Are you** John Crow from British Inland?

Identifying yourself

> **I'm** John Crow **from** British Inland.
> **My name is** Osorio da Silva. **I'm** the Technical Sales Manager at AMB.

Introducing other people

> **Let me introduce** | my colleague, Peter Burnell.
> **I'd like you to meet** |
>
> **He's our** new Purchasing Manager.
>
> **This is** Paulo Santos, **head of** AMB's Overseas Sales Division.

Greetings for first meetings

Greeting	Reply
How do you do?	**How do you do?**
(I'm) pleased to meet you.	**Very pleased to meet you, too.**

Greetings for second and subsequent meetings

Greeting	Reply
It's | **good** | **to see you again.** **nice**	**(It's)** | **good** | **to see you again, too.** **nice**
How are you?	**Very well, thanks. And you?**

A3 Tasks

I. A Dutch visitor is waiting in the reception area of the British Inland offices in Manchester.

The seven lines below are from a conversation between him and two British Inland employees. Put them in the correct order.

Follow the example.

a. Pleased to meet you, Mr Wood.
b. That's right.
c. Very pleased to meet you, too.

START ➔ d. Excuse me. Are you Mr Van de Kleu? (I)

e. How do you do?
f. Mr Van de Kleu, I'd like you to meet Paul Wood from our Sales Department.
g. How do you do? I'm John Crow, the General Manager.

Check your answers in the key A3.I

10 ■

2. What would you say in the following situations?

Follow the example.

Situation	Your words
a. You meet an ex-colleague at a conference. Greet her.	*It's nice to see you again. How are you?*
b. You go down to the reception area of your company to meet Hans Becker. You haven't met him before. Check his identity.	
c. Greet Mr Becker.	
d. You want to introduce your colleague John Kay, the Data Processing Manager, to Mr Becker.	
e. You meet a business contact by chance at the airport. He asks how you are. Reply.	

Compare your answers with those recorded on tape **A3.2**

B Interaction – How to keep a conversation moving

B1 Focus

In order to establish a good atmosphere, it is important to keep the conversation moving and to show interest in what the other side has to say.

Listen to tape B1. You will now hear a continuation of the previous conversation in the hotel bar.

1. Decide if the following statements are *true* or *false*.
   a. The visitors are unwilling to try Brazilian food or drink.
   b. The conversation flows easily, without silences or hesitations.
   c. The visitors show interest in learning about Brazil.
   d. The Brazilians ask most of the questions.

Check your answers in the key **B1.1**

2. Listen to tape B1 again and complete the missing words in the extracts. Then read the notes on the right.

	Extract 1	*Notes*
PAULO SANTOS	This .... to Brazil, ... , Peter?	*Asks a question*
PETER BURNELL	.... Unfortunately, this is only a short visit, so we won't be able to see very much.	*Answers* *Adds a comment*
PAULO SANTOS	.... , and it is a very large country.	*Reacts* *Adds a comment*

Extract 2

Notes

PETER BURNELL This really is very good.

.... it a lot? *Asks a question*

OSORIO DA SILVA .... *Caipirinha* is very popular. *Answers*
And of course, we also drink a lot of beer in Brazil. *Adds information*

PETER BURNELL .... ? *Shows interest*

And .... brewed here or mainly imported? *Asks a related question*

OSORIO DA SILVA We mainly drink Brazilian beers and some of them *Answers*

.... *Adds a comment*

JOHN CROW And .... ? *Asks a question*

PAULO SANTOS We .... too, *Answers*
especially in the very south near Uruguay. But in general, *Adds information*
we produce and drink less wine than Argentina, for example.

JOHN CROW .... *Shows interest*

What's .... ? *Asks a related question*

Check your answers in the key **B1.2**

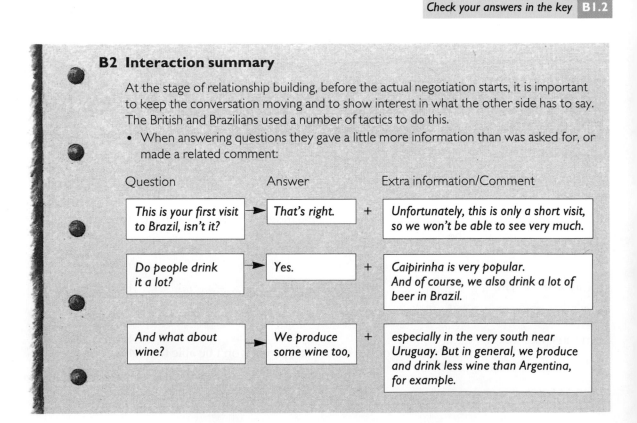

B2 Interaction summary

At the stage of relationship building, before the actual negotiation starts, it is important to keep the conversation moving and to show interest in what the other side has to say. The British and Brazilians used a number of tactics to do this.

- When answering questions they gave a little more information than was asked for, or made a related comment:

Question	Answer	Extra information/Comment
This is your first visit to Brazil, isn't it? →	*That's right.* +	*Unfortunately, this is only a short visit, so we won't be able to see very much.*
Do people drink it a lot? →	*Yes.* +	*Caipirinha is very popular. And of course, we also drink a lot of beer in Brazil.*
And what about wine? →	*We produce some wine too,* +	*especially in the very south near Uruguay. But in general, we produce and drink less wine than Argentina, for example.*

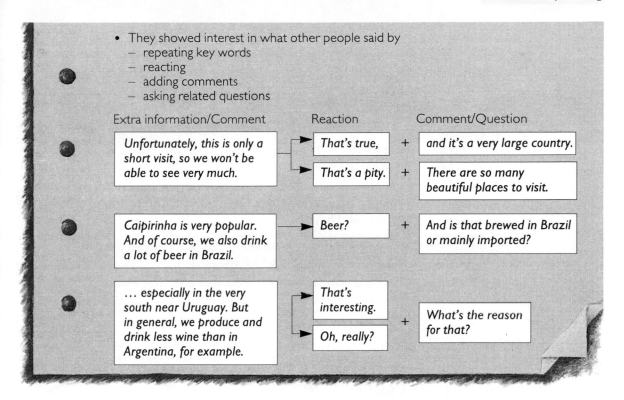

- They showed interest in what other people said by
  - repeating key words
  - reacting
  - adding comments
  - asking related questions

Extra information/Comment	Reaction		Comment/Question
Unfortunately, this is only a short visit, so we won't be able to see very much.	*That's true,*	+	*and it's a very large country.*
	That's a pity.	+	*There are so many beautiful places to visit.*
Caipirinha is very popular. And of course, we also drink a lot of beer in Brazil.	*Beer?*	+	*And is that brewed in Brazil or mainly imported?*
... especially in the very south near Uruguay. But in general, we produce and drink less wine than in Argentina, for example.	*That's interesting.*	+	*What's the reason for that?*
	Oh, really?		

B3 Tasks

1. The questions and answers below come from a conversation between John Crow and a French supplier in Toulouse. Match each question with an answer and comment/extra information.

Follow the example.

Question	Answer	Comment/Extra information
a. People drink quite a lot of wine in France, don't they?	Yes,	It's my first visit, but I was in Bordeaux a couple of years ago.
b. Have you been to Toulouse before?	Just two days.	but the amount has dropped in recent years.
c. Are you staying here long?	That's a good idea.	In fact, I do a bit of French cooking myself.
d. Would you like to eat outside?	Very much.	Then I have to go to Paris.
e. Do you like French food?	No.	It's still very warm.

Check your answers in the key **B3.1**

2. Now you are going to respond to the comments and extra information given in task B3.1.

Listen to tape B3.2. First you will hear John Crow or the French supplier answering a question and making a comment. Respond following the written instruction. Then you will hear a model version.

Follow the example.

a. Example

John Crow	Just two days. Then I have to go to Paris.
Instruction	React and comment.
You	....
Model version	**That's a pity. You won't have much time to look round Toulouse, then.**

b.	Instruction	Repeat key words to show interest and ask a related question.
c.	Instruction	Show interest and ask a related question.
d.	Instruction	React and make a comment about the recent hot weather.
e.	Instruction	Show interest and ask a related question.

C Style – What to call people

CI Focus

I. Listen to tape CI. You will hear an extract from one of the dialogues that you listened to earlier in this unit.

Compare it with the written version below.

SANTOS	Mr Crow, it's good to see you again. How are you?
CROW	Hello, Mr Santos. Very well, thanks.

What difference do you notice in the use of names?

Check your answers in the key **CI.I**

2. Now put a tick (✔) in one (or more) of the boxes below.

The version written in C1.1 above is:

a. more formal ☐

b. more polite ☐ than the version on tape C1.

c. more appropriate ☐

Compare your ideas with those in the key **C1.2**

3. The extract below is another version of the first meeting between Paulo Santos and Peter Burnell. Read it, then answer the questions below.

SANTOS I'm pleased to meet you, Mr Burnell.
BURNELL Very pleased to meet you, too, Paulo.

Do you think:

	Probably	Probably not
a. Santos says 'Mr Burnell' because the British man is a potential customer?	☐	☐
b. Burnell says 'Paulo' in order to underline his own position of strength as a potential customer?	☐	☐
c. Burnell wants to move to a first name basis in order to establish an atmosphere of informality?	☐	☐

Compare your ideas with those in the key **C1.3**

C2 Style summary

There is, of course, no standard approach to the use of names. There are wide variations from individual to individual and from culture to culture. For example, within their own cultures, Germans and Japanese will rarely use first names outside circles of family and close friends; North Americans, Swedes and the Spanish will generally move to first names at an early stage in a business relationship.

At the initial meeting stage, it is clearly important to create a climate in which all participants feel comfortable. In the international context this will almost certainly mean some adjusting and compromise.

If you are unsure of how the people you are meeting will deal with names:

- Introduce yourself and others by giving the full name.
  I'm Marion Black. *(not I'm Mrs Black.)*
  This is Yoshi Kitawara. *(not This is Mr Kitawara.)*

- If the other person is your host, listen to how he/she uses your name.
  Pleased to meet you, Tom. ➤ **Pleased to meet you, too, Rafael.**
  How do you do, Mrs Black? ➤ **How do you do, Mr Kitawara?**

- If you think using first names will be acceptable, suggest this.
  By the way, please call me Peter.

C3 Task

Rewrite the dialogue below to make the use of names *clear* and *consistent*. Person B is the host.

A: Tom, I'd like you to meet my friend Hari Ponnambalam.
    Hari and I used to do business together in Sri Lanka.
    Hari, this is Mr Jenkins, head of the Marketing Department.
B: I'm pleased to meet you, Hari.
C: Pleased to meet you, too, Mr Jenkins.

| Check your answers in the key | C3 |

D Cross-cultural differences – What would you do?

D1 Focus

It's important to remember that different people do things in different ways. This is partly a question of individual style. However, we often make *assumptions* based on the way things are done in *our culture*. Sometimes these may be rather different from the other sides' assumptions.

Check some of your assumptions here. Put a tick (✔) in the Yes or No column in each case.

	Yes	No
1. The negotiation itself is of prime importance. It is also important to socialise but this can be done after an agreement has been reached.		
2. If possible, I like to get to know a potential business partner in a neutral and relaxed environment, for example, at a restaurant.		
3. I hand over my business card in the first few moments.		
4. On meeting a negotiating partner, I usually shake hands and at the same time put my other hand on his shoulder.		
5. I try to prepare for the relationship building stage by finding out in advance which topics might be controversial.		

Now read the cross-cultural summary below for a comment on each assumption.

D2 Cross-cultural summary

1. Different cultures place varying degrees of emphasis on the importance of relationship building. For example, in many Middle Eastern countries no business can be done until a relationship of mutual trust and confidence has gradually been built up between the two parties. By contrast, in Finland, small talk before a negotiation is generally kept to a minimum, and most of the relationship building will take place afterwards, in a restaurant or sauna.

2. In many cultures people find it easier to build a relationship with a potential business partner in a social setting. This is particularly true of many European cultures, such as Spain, France and the UK.

3. The practice of immediately handing over a business card is probably most common among the Japanese. It has the advantage of helping you to remember unfamiliar names and to understand better the role and status of the members of the other negotiating team. However, in other cultures, for example, Germany, it's more common to exchange business cards at the end of a meeting.

4. The amount of touching which is acceptable in different cultures also shows great variation and, of course, varies within cultures depending on the gender of the participants. In general, Latin American cultures permit more physical contact between men than, for example, Anglo-Saxon cultures. The distance at which two people stand from each other also differs. In Latin American and Arab cultures, people generally stand closer together when talking than Europeans or Americans do.

5. It is certainly prudent to avoid controversial topics at this stage of the negotiation. However, the conventional 'taboo' topics of politics and religion may be acceptable if you concentrate on information-gathering type questions (*who/what/how*?) rather than questions which imply comment or criticism. For example, 'How is your President elected?' rather than 'Why does your President have such a long term of office?'

The notes above are intended as a general guide only, and should not be taken as an indication of the way every person from any of the cultures mentioned will behave.

Answer key

A Language

A1.1

a. False b. False c. True d. False

A1 🔊

DA SILVA: Excuse me. **Are you** Mr Crow and Mr Burnell from British Inland?

CROW: That's right. **I'm** John Crow, and **this is** Peter Burnell.

DA SILVA: **How do you do? My name is** Osorio da Silva. **I'm the Technical Sales Manager** at AMB.

CROW: How do you do?

BURNELL: Pleased to meet you.

DA SILVA: So, welcome to Brazil! You must be tired after your long journey.

BURNELL: No, not too tired. We've had most of the day to relax, and the hotel is very comfortable.

DA SILVA: Good. Paulo Santos will be joining us in the bar in ten or fifteen minutes. Then we plan to go to a restaurant. So can I offer you a drink?

CROW: Good idea …

DA SILVA: Ah, here's Paulo now.

SANTOS: **John**, it's **good to see you again**. How **are you**?

CROW: **Hello**, Paulo. **Very well, thanks.** It's **nice to be here** in Brazil. Rather a change from Manchester.

SANTOS: Oh, yes. That was a bit too cold for me last December!

CROW: **Let me introduce my colleague,** Peter Burnell. **He's our** new **Purchasing Manager.** Peter, **this is** Paulo Santos, **head of** AMB's Overseas Sales Division.

SANTOS: **I'm pleased to meet you**, Mr Burnell.

BURNELL: **Very pleased to meet you,** too.

A1.2

See tapescript A1 above. The missing words are in **bold**.

A3.1

1. d 2. b 3. g 4. e 5. f 6. a 7. c

A3.2 🔊 Model version

a. It's nice to see you again. How are you?

b. Excuse me. Are you Mr Becker?

c. How do you do, Mr Becker?
   or
   I'm pleased to meet you, Mr Becker.

d. Mr Becker, I'd like you to meet my colleague, John Kay. He's our Data Processing Manager.
   or
   Mr Becker, let me introduce my colleague, John Kay, head of our Data Processing Department.

e. Very well, thanks. And you?

B Interaction

B1.1

a. False b. True c. True d. False

B1 🔊

SANTOS: Would you like another drink? Have you tried *Caipirinha* yet?

CROW: I don't think so. What is it ?

SANTOS: It's a cocktail based on a drink made from sugar cane.

CROW: That sounds good.

SANTOS: And for you, Mr Burnell?

BURNELL: I'll try that too. By the way, please call me Peter.

SANTOS: Good, and I'm Paulo, as you know. Osorio, would you like *Caipirinha* too?

DA SILVA: Yes.

SANTOS: *Por favor, quatro Caipirinhas.*

SANTOS: Here we are. Cheers, or *Saude* as we say.

BURNELL: Cheers.

CROW: *Saude.* Mmm – it's very good.

SANTOS: This **is your first visit** to Brazil, **isn't it,** Peter?

BURNELL: **That's right.** Unfortunately, this is only a short visit, so we won't be able to see very much.

SANTOS: **That's true**, and it is a very large country. But we'll certainly try to show you something of the city. And I hope, anyway, that this will be the first of many visits.

CROW: Indeed. So do we. Maybe next time it'll be possible to add a few days' holiday to the trip.

BURNELL: This really is very good. **Do people drink** it a lot?

DA SILVA: **Yes.** *Caipirinha* is very popular. And of course, we also drink a lot of beer in Brazil.

BURNELL: **Beer?** And **is that** brewed here or mainly imported?

DA SILVA: We mainly drink Brazilian beers and some of them **are very good**.

CROW: And **what about wine?**

SANTOS: We **produce some wine** too, especially in the very south near Uruguay. But in general, we produce and drink less wine than Argentina, for example.

CROW: **That's interesting**. What's **the reason for that?**

SANTOS: Basically it's too hot. A lot of the country is tropical and sub-tropical and that's not a good climate for producing wine.

B1.2

See tapescript B1 above. The missing words are in **bold**.

B3.1

a. Yes, but the amount has dropped in recent years.
b. No. It's my first visit, but I was in Bordeaux a couple of years ago.
c. Just two days. Then I have to go to Paris.
d. That's a good idea. It's still very warm.
e. Very much. In fact, I do a bit of French cooking myself.

B3.2

a. (Example)
Crow: Just two days. Then I have to go to Paris.
You: ....
Model version: **That's a pity. You won't have much time to look round Toulouse, then.**
b. Crow: No. It's my first visit, but I was in Bordeaux a couple of years ago.
You: ....
Model version: **Ah, in Bordeaux? Were you on holiday there?**
c. French supplier: Yes, but the amount has dropped in recent years.
You: ....
Model version: **Oh, really? What's the reason for that?**
or
That's interesting. Do you think that's for health reasons?

d. Crow: That's a good idea. It's still very warm.
You: ....
Model version: **That's true. We've been having very hot weather recently.**
e. Crow: Very much. In fact I do a bit of French cooking myself.
You: ....
Model version: **Oh, really? Where did you learn that?**
or
Oh, really? Is it common for British men to cook?

C Style

C1.1

On tape C1, both speakers use each other's first names. Here they use surnames.

C1

SANTOS: John, it's good to see you again. How are you?
CROW: Hello, Paulo. Very well, thanks.

C1.2

a. Note that politeness is not necessarily related to formality. The use of first names in this context was not impolite or inappropriate, as both speakers had met before and, presumably, agreed to be on first name terms.

C1.3

a. Probably not. It's more likely he says this because, in Brazil, surnames are usually used on first meetings in business situations.
b. Probably not. There is no other evidence that he is trying to do this.
c. Probably. In Britain first names are often used in business situations, and an informal style is not uncommon.

C3

A: Tom, I'd like you to meet my friend Hari Ponnambalam.
Hari and I used to do business together in Sri Lanka.
Hari, this is **Tom Jenkins**, head of the Marketing Department.
B: I'm pleased to meet you, Hari.
C: Pleased to meet you, too, **Tom**.

Agreeing procedure

A	Language	How to introduce and check acceptance of objectives
B	Interaction	How to create a climate of cooperation
C	Style	How to make suggestions and statements less direct
D	Cross-cultural differences	What's going wrong?

Background

This is a continuation of the scenario in Unit 1, in which two managers from the airline, British Inland, are visiting Brazil to have preliminary negotiations with Aircraft Manufacturers of Brazil (AMB) about the purchase of aircraft. This unit covers the early part of their first formal meeting.

A Language – How to introduce and check acceptance of objectives

A1 Focus

At the beginning of the negotiation it is important for both sides to agree on the overall objectives and procedure. This will ensure that nothing is forgotten or left out, and that both sides have a clear idea of the agenda.

Listen to tape A1. You will now hear the opening part of a meeting between John Crow and Peter Burnell of British Inland, and Paulo Santos of AMB.

1. Decide if the following statements are *true* or *false*.
   a. The Brazilians already have a detailed plan for the next three days.
   b. Paulo Santos already knows enough about the British company's needs.
   c. In this meeting the British side wants to find out as much as possible about AMB's products.
   d. Price will also be an item on the agenda.

   Check your answers in the key A1.1

2. Listen to tape A1 again and complete the missing words in the extracts. Then read the notes on the right.

Extract 1

Notes

PAULO SANTOS Can we now ....

.... for the next three days?

Asks for agreement on procedure

I'd like to check ....

....

Checks the other side's objectives

Obviously, ... is to find out more about your airline's needs and then talk about ways in which we would be able to service those needs.

States his side's principal objectives

Does that ....

.... ?

Checks that this is acceptable to the other side

Extract 2

JOHN CROW ... we're already very interested in your aircraft.

....

.... from this meeting is a full picture of your current products' capabilities, your development plans, and how these aspects match our needs.

States his side's principal objective

....

.... possible pricing, delivery and support arrangements.

States supplementary objectives

Check your answers in the key A1.2

A2 Language summary

At the opening stage of the meeting it is important to state the objectives clearly and to agree on them with the other party.

Getting agreement on procedure

Can we now agree on the overall procedure?
First of all, I think we should establish the overall procedure.

Stating principal objectives

Our main objective is to ...

| **What we'd like to** | **achieve** | **from this meeting is ...** |
| | **get** | |

Stating supplementary objectives

We'd also like to talk about ...
Another objective, as we see it, is ...
Something else we'd like to achieve is ...

Checking agreement and acceptance of objectives

Does that fit in with your objectives?
Is that OK with you?
Does that seem acceptable to you?

A3 Tasks

I. Expand the notes below into an introduction and statement of objectives. Follow the example.

a. Example

1. Get agreement on procedure
2. State principal objective: exchange of ideas

Model version **Can we now agree on the overall procedure? What we'd like to achieve from this meeting is an exchange of ideas.**

(You can hear this model version recorded on tape A3.1.)

b. 1. Get agreement on procedure
   2. State principal objective: identify areas of common interest

c. 1. Get agreement on procedure
   2. State principal objective: review of progress so far

d. 1. Get agreement on procedure
   2. State principal objective: find out more about your product range

e. 1. Get agreement on procedure
   2. State principal objective: clear understanding of each other's research capabilities

Now listen to the model versions on tape A3.1.

2. The following sentences all state a supplementary objective and then check the other side's agreement. Complete the gaps in the sentences.

Follow the example.

a. We'd ....*also*........*like*........*to*........*talk*........*about*........ other areas for possible cooperation. ....*Is*........*that*........*OK*........ with you?

b. ...., as we see it, ... to agree on a preliminary time schedule. Does .... you?

c. Something .... is agreement on a new pricing formula. .... your objectives?

d. .... also .... about manpower requirements. Is .... ?

Check your answers in the key **A3.2**

B Interaction – How to create a climate of cooperation

BI Focus

Most negotiations work better when both sides cooperate to reach mutually beneficial agreements. You can create this climate of cooperation at the early stages of a negotiation by seeking positive responses to relatively small points.

🔊 Listen to tape B1. You will now hear another extract from the same meeting.

1. Answer the following questions.
  a. The two sides have reached broad agreement on objectives. What do they now want to agree on?
  b. What do both sides feel should be:

  the first item on the agenda? ....

  the second item on the agenda? ....

  the third item on the agenda? ....

Check your answers in the key `B1.1`

🔊 **2.** Listen to tape B1 again and complete the missing words in the extract. Then read the notes on the right.

Extract	Notes
PAULO SANTOS Good. We seem to have broad agreement on objectives.	
.... the order in which we want to talk about things?	*Asks for agreement on the agenda*
JOHN CROW	*Gives positive response*
PAULO SANTOS Well, ... by looking at your situation and your needs. .... with that?	*Makes suggestion* *Asks for agreement*
JOHN CROW Yes, ... We'd be happy to start with that.	*Gives positive response*
PAULO SANTOS We .... to a presentation of our family of aircraft, and our range of customer services.	*Makes suggestion*
.... ?	*Asks for agreement*
PETER BURNELL .... , ... We'd also be very interested in visiting your factory at an early stage of the proceedings, if possible.	*Agrees*
PAULO SANTOS Certainly. We were thinking of taking you to visit our production and test facilities tomorrow. .... your plans?	*Asks for agreement*
JOHN CROW Yes, ...	*Agrees*

Check your answers in the key `B1.2`

B2 Interaction summary

In this early phase of a negotiation, it is generally important to create *a climate of cooperation*. The participants in the British Inland/AMB meeting used a number of tactics to achieve this.

- The British visitors were asked to agree on items of procedure when it was almost certain they would agree.
- This climate of agreement and cooperation was strengthened by the use of positive responses by the other side.

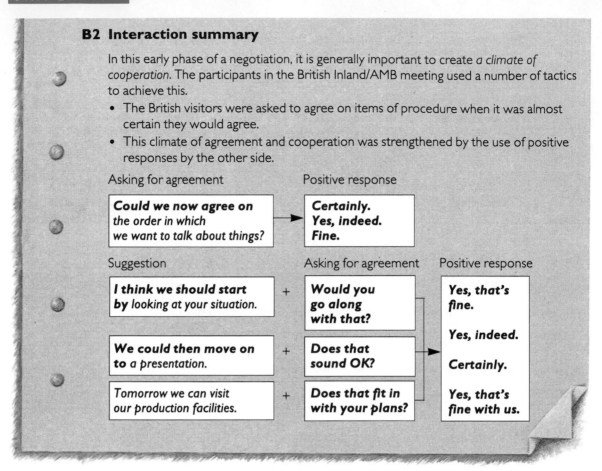

Asking for agreement

Could we now agree on the order in which we want to talk about things?

Positive response

Certainly.
Yes, indeed.
Fine.

Suggestion

I think we should start by looking at your situation.

We could then move on to a presentation.

Tomorrow we can visit our production facilities.

Asking for agreement

Would you go along with that?

+

Does that sound OK?

+

Does that fit in with your plans?

+

Positive response

Yes, that's fine.

Yes, indeed.

Certainly.

Yes, that's fine with us.

B3 Tasks

1. These are nine exchanges from the early stage of a negotiation between a buyer and a supplier. Put them in the correct order. The buyer speaks first.

Follow the example.

Phrases from the negotiation

a. Yes, that's a good idea. And while we're on that subject, I'd also like to talk about delivery costs. Is that OK with you?

b. Certainly.

c. Fine. We'll make that the third item then.

d. Right. Well, what's most important for us is the question of quality control, so I think we should start by discussing that. Would you go along with that?

e. We'd then like to talk about delivery schedules. Does that sound OK?

f. OK. So we could spend the first half hour on that topic. Is that OK with you?

START → g. Could we now agree on the order in which we want to talk about things?   (1)

h. That's fine with me.

i. Yes, indeed. We've just introduced new quality control procedures, so that's very relevant.

Check your answers in the key **B3.1**

2. You are a buyer. You are going to agree the agenda for a negotiation with a supplier. His part of the discussion is on the tape. Study the interaction plan and prepare what you want to say.

🔲 When you are ready, listen to tape B3.2 and play the role of the buyer.

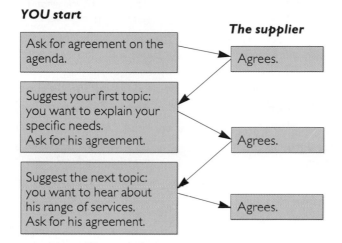

YOU start

The supplier

🔲 Now listen to the complete interaction on tape B3.3.

C Style – How to make suggestions and statements less direct

C1 Focus

1. Listen to tape C1. You will hear four short extracts from one of the dialogues that you listened to earlier in the unit. After each extract, stop the tape and compare the recorded version with the version in column A below. Write down the words used on the tape which correspond to the words in *italics*.

Follow the example.

A	Taped version
a. *It is time to start.*	I think we should start.
b. *Now we must agree* on the overall procedure.	
c. *I want to check* what you hope to achieve.	
d. *We also need to talk* about prices.	

Check your answers in the key `C1.1`

2. Now put a a tick (✓) in one of the boxes below.

The versions in column A are:

a. more direct than ☐

b. more polite than ☐   the versions on tape C1.

c. almost the same as ☐

Compare your ideas with those in the key `C1.2`

C2 Style summary

To create the strongest climate of cooperation in a negotiation, there are certain choices about the *style* of language which can be made.

- Use of *would like* to make requests sound *less direct*.

I want to check what you hope to achieve. ⟶ **I'd like** to check what you hope to achieve.

- Use of *should, could, might, would* to make statements and suggestions sound *less dogmatic*. It is also better to introduce suggestions with phrases such as *I think, maybe, perhaps*.

It is time to start our meeting. ⟶ **I think we should start** our meeting.

I'll outline our objectives. ⟶ **Perhaps I could** outline our objectives.

- Use of *questions* to make suggestions in a less direct way.

Now we must agree on the overall procedure. ⟶ **Can we now agree** on the overall procedure?

The less direct and less dogmatic choices are particularly useful when dealing with people who are native speakers of English, for whom a direct and forceful style may be interpreted as a sign of aggressive behaviour.

> Remember that this style summary gives you *choices*. There will be occasions when you want to be direct and will choose appropriate language to show this!

C3 Task

Look at the statements below. They could be used at the beginning of a negotiation to establish the procedure of the meeting. In each case they are very direct. Give a version which is less direct, and will help to create a better climate of cooperation. Follow the example.

Example

a. We'll talk about price. *I think we should talk about price.*

b. I want to hear about delivery procedures.

c. We'll deal with penalty clauses tomorrow.

d. We have to finish the meeting at 5.00 pm.

e. We want your ideas on this.

f. We'll look at the specifications tomorrow.

g. I'll summarise our objectives.

Check your answers in the key **C3**

D Cross-cultural differences – What's going wrong?

D1 Focus

Listen to tape D1. You will hear a short extract from a meeting. On one side there are two representatives of Setel, a US company producing software systems for use in production processes in the optical fibre industry. On the other side are two representatives of Nippon Glass, a Japanese electric glass manufacturer.

The comments below were made after the meeting by various members of the negotiating teams.

If you think a comment was made by an American, put **A** in the column. Put **J** if you think it was made by one of the Japanese. In each case give your reason.

Comment	A / J	Reason
a. I get the impression they don't like us.		
b. Why are they telling us obvious things?		
c. They're very sales-oriented.		
d. I've no idea what they're really thinking.		

Compare your ideas with those in the key **D1**

D2 Cross-cultural summary

The reaction of people to the style of this meeting will depend on their cultural perspective. It is probable that the American participants in the discussion will feel that the Japanese are far too silent, suggesting that they are unhappy about something, or that they do not want to be cooperative. From their side, the Japanese may feel that the Americans are talking too much, and asking unnecessary questions.

In American culture, meaning is mainly conveyed through words – so people speak a lot to express what they feel and think. Relatively little is left to be understood from the context, where what is *not* said is as important as what is said. In some other cultures, a lot of meaning is contained in situations and contexts, and words may be less necessary. People from such cultures are, therefore, often considered to be rather silent and uncommunicative. But, in reality, the communication is taking place in an unspoken way.

Answer key

A Language

A1.1

a. False b. False c. True d. True

A1 ▭

SANTOS: I think we should start. First of all, I'd like to say that we hope that this will be the beginning of a good business relationship for both our companies.

CROW: Yes, indeed. So do we.

SANTOS: Good. Can we now **agree on the overall procedure** for the next three days? I'd like to check **what you hope to achieve**. Obviously, **our main objective** is to find out more about your airline's needs and then talk about ways in which we would be able to service those needs. Does that **fit in with your objectives?**

CROW: Yes, that's very much how we see it too. The fact that we're here means that we're already very interested in your aircraft. **What we'd like to get** from this meeting is a full picture of your current products' capabilities, your development plans, and how these aspects match our needs. **We'd also like to talk about** possible pricing, delivery and support arrangements.

SANTOS: Good. We seem to have broad agreement on objectives.

A1.2

See tapescript A1 above. The missing words are in **bold**.

A3.1 ▭ Model version

a. (Example) Can we now agree on the overall procedure? What we'd like to achieve from this meeting is an exchange of ideas.

b. Can we now agree on the overall procedure? Our main objective is to identify areas of common interest.

c. First of all, I think we should establish the overall procedure. What we'd like to get from this meeting is a review of progress so far.

d. First of all, I think we should establish the overall procedure. Our main objective is to find out more about your product range.

e. Can we now agree on the overall procedure? What we'd like to achieve from this meeting is a clear understanding of each other's research capabilities.

A3.2

b. **Another objective**, as we see it, **is** to agree on a preliminary time schedule. Does **that seem acceptable to** you?

c. Something **else we'd like to achieve** is agreement on a new pricing formula. **Does that fit in with** your objectives?

d. **We'd** also **like to talk** about manpower requirements. Is **that OK with you?**

B Interaction

B1.1

a. The order in which to talk about the topics.

b. first: British Inland's needs
second: AMB's aircraft and range of services
third: visit to AMB's production and test facilities

B1 ▭

SANTOS: Good. We seem to have broad agreement on objectives. **Could we now agree on** the order in which we want to talk about things?

CROW: **Certainly.**

SANTOS: Well, **I think we should start** by looking at your situation and your needs. **Would you go along** with that?

CROW: Yes, **that's fine.** We'd be happy to start with that.

SANTOS: We **could then move on** to a presentation of our family of aircraft, and our range of customer services. **Does that sound OK?**

BURNELL: **Yes, indeed.** We'd also be very interested in visiting your factory at an early stage of the proceedings, if possible.

SANTOS: Certainly. We were thinking of taking you to visit our production and test facilities tomorrow. **Does that fit in with** your plans?

CROW: Yes, **that's fine with us.**

B1.2

See tapescript B1 above. The missing words are in **bold**.

B3.1

1. g   2. b   3. d   4. i   5. f   6. h   7. e   8. a   9. c

B3.2 📼

YOU: ....
SUPPLIER: Certainly.
YOU: ....
SUPPLIER: That's fine with me.
YOU: ....
SUPPLIER: Yes, that's fine.

B3.3 📼 Complete interaction

BUYER: **Could we now agree on the order in which we want to talk about things?**
SUPPLIER: Certainly.
BUYER: **I think we should start by explaining our specific needs. Would you go along with that?**
SUPPLIER: That's fine with me.
BUYER: **Good. I'd then like to hear about your range of services. Does that sound OK?**
SUPPLIER: Yes, that's fine.

C Style

C1.1

b. Can we now agree … ?
c. I'd like to check …
d. We'd also like to talk …

C1 📼

Extract 1
SANTOS: I think we should start. First of all, …
Extract 2
SANTOS: Good. Can we now agree on the overall procedure for the next three days?
Extract 3
SANTOS: I'd like to check what you hope to achieve.
Extract 4
CROW: … and how these aspects match our needs. We'd also like to talk about possible pricing, delivery, and support arrangements.

C1.2

a.

C3 Model version

b. I'd like to hear about delivery procedures.

c. Can we deal with penalty clauses tomorrow?
d. I think we should finish the meeting at 5.00 pm.
e. We'd like to have your ideas on this.
f. Could we look at the specifications tomorrow?
g. Perhaps I could summarise our objectives.

D Cross-cultural differences

D1

a. A Silence makes Americans feel uncomfortable and can sometimes be seen as threatening.
b. J To the Japanese it's unnecessary to talk through the thinking process.
c. J The Japanese don't appreciate a 'hard sell' approach.
d. A Americans expect more verbal feedback.

D1 📼

BILL: As George was remarking, our latest software control systems are proving very popular with both medium and large-sized manufacturers.
GEORGE: That's right – our US and Canadian customers are particularly pleased with the flexibility they offer. And, as I understand from you, Takashi, one of the main purposes of your visit is to look at how our range of software would suit your developing needs in the optical fibre area.
Silence
Bill, would you like to run through the day's programme at this stage?
BILL: Sure. But first, have you guys got any questions? Yeah, Akira?
Silence
AKIRA: No, everything is clear.
BILL: Oh, OK. George.
GEORGE: Thanks, Bill. As you can see on the programme in front of you, I will first be making a short presentation of our product range, concentrating on the new control systems. Then there is a space for you to present to us your future needs at Nippon Glass and how we at Setel may be able to help you. We will then be breaking for lunch. After lunch we plan to go to our facility in which you will see the new system, as well as some of our other products, in operation. How does that programme sound to you?
Silence
TAKASHI: It's fine. We are here because we are interested in your software system.
Silence
GEORGE: Well, Takashi, we think you will be even more interested by the end of the day …

Exchanging information

A	*Language*	How to make opening statements
B	*Interaction*	How to check understanding
C	*Style*	How to be clear and maintain cooperation
D	*Cross-cultural differences*	What's going wrong?

Background

Italchimica S.p.A. is an Italian chemical company. One of their major products is titanium dioxide, which is used in the manufacture of paints and paper. H M Griggs Inc. is a large American producer of paints. The company is considering using Italchimica to supply some of its titanium dioxide needs.

The International Sales Manager from Italchimica is visiting the Griggs headquarters in Pittsburgh to discuss a possible deal.

A Language – How to make opening statements

A1 Focus

After establishing a climate of cooperation and agreeing procedure, the next step is to make a clear opening statement.

Listen to tape A1. You will now hear an early part of the meeting between Italchimica and H M Griggs.

Taking part in the meeting are

Luigi Frigerio	International Sales Manager, Italchimica
Tom Hall	Purchasing Manager, H M Griggs

1. Decide if the following statements are *true* or *false*.
   a. They are going to discuss the procedure for the meeting in this session.
   b. The American company has been operating for more than 50 years.
   c. Originally H M Griggs was active only in the domestic market.
   d. H M Griggs plans to expand its export market by buying European companies.
   e. Griggs wishes to replace its existing supplier of titanium dioxide.
   f. Finding a second supplier of titanium dioxide for the US market is the most important issue.

Check your answers in the key A1.1

2. Listen to tape A1 again and complete the missing words in the extracts.
Then read the notes on the right.

Extract 1

Notes

TOM HALL   Well, H M Griggs .... in 1922.

We .... high quality decorative and industrial paints.

.... , we are the fifth largest US paint producer with

an .... of over $5 billion. In 1982 we

started an export division and exports ....

.... 20 per cent of our turnover.

Talks about the history and general activities of the company.
Talks about the present situation

Extract 2

TOM HALL   ... to the more immediate reason for our meeting today,

....
increasing our options for supply of titanium dioxide.

States his general negotiating interest

Extract 3

TOM HALL   However, in line with our export expansion and foreign acquisition
plans, especially in Europe, we'd like to work with a supplier who
has experience and a presence in the European market.

.... here is easy access to
supplies.

This is .... to us.

Our domestic market, here in the US, is also expanding, and
for this market we are also interested in looking for a second

supplier but at the moment this is ....

.... to us.

States a specific interest

Emphasises it

States a less important interest

Check your answers in the key   **A1.2**

A2 Language summary

A clear *opening statement* enables the participants in the negotiation to understand the background and interests of each party. It often:

- begins with a short summary of the company's history and activities.
- moves on to statements of each side's interests.

Talking about the history and general activities of the company

| H M Griggs | *was founded was set up* | *in 1922.* |
| We | *manufacture produce supply* | *high quality paints.* |

Talking about the present situation

Currently, we are the fifth largest US paint producer.
We have an annual turnover of over $5 billion.
Exports now account for 20 per cent of our turnover.

Stating general negotiating interests

We're interested in increasing our options ...
We'd like to work with a supplier who ...

Stating and emphasising specific negotiating interests

Our key interest here is ...
... is extremely important to us
It's vital for us to ...
It's imperative for us to ...

Stating less important interests

... is of lesser importance to us.
... is a lower priority.

A3 Tasks

I. Look at the company profile below. Talk about the company's history and activities.

1851	Robert Duval founded the Duval Telegraph Company in Paris.
Nowadays	Duval S.A. is world leader in electrical and electronic engineering.
Activities	Telecommunications networks, information systems, electrical installation, components
Factories	15 countries worldwide
Employees	200,000 worldwide
Turnover	$20 billion last year

Compare your version with the one recorded on tape A3.1

2. Expand the notes below into spoken opening statements. Follow the example.

a. **Example**

General interest	expanding into Far Eastern markets
Specific interest	agency for our products in Taiwan
Less important interest	mainland Chinese market

Model version **We're interested in expanding into Far Eastern markets. Our key interest here is to set up an agency for our products in Taiwan. We'd also like to explore the mainland Chinese market, but this is a lower priority.**

(You can hear this model version recorded on tape A3.2.)

b.
General interest	establishing a US subsidiary
Specific interest	increase market penetration in US
Less important interest	Canada

c.
General interest	working with supplier with experience of offshore platforms
Specific interest	supplier has North Sea experience
Less important interest	advanced design techniques

d.
General interest	diversifying our activities
Specific interest	develop services with higher added value
Less important interest	adapt products for international market

Compare your version with the one recorded on tape **A3.2**

B Interaction – How to check understanding

B1 Focus

To avoid misunderstanding later in the negotiation, it is important to check that you have understood the main points the other side has made.

Listen to tape B1. You will now hear a second extract from the same meeting.

1. Answer the following questions.

i. When Tom Hall finishes his opening statement, does Luigi Frigerio then:

   a. explain his own negotiating interests?

   b. ask questions to get more information from Tom Hall?

   c. repeat key points from Tom Hall's opening statement?

   d. none of these?

ii. From the information which Luigi Frigerio gives, does Italchimica seem to be a suitable supplier to meet H M Griggs needs?

Check your answers in the key **B1.1**

2. Listen to tape B1 again and complete the missing words in the extracts. Then read the notes on the right.

Extract 1   *Notes*

LUIGI FRIGERIO   Sure. ....   *Signals that he*
recap on your main points first, and then I can tell you how   *wants to recap*
I think Italchimica might be able to help you.

TOM HALL   Fine – good idea.

LUIGI FRIGERIO So, ... *Leads in to key points*
H M Griggs is planning an expansion into Europe ...

Extract 2

LUIGI FRIGERIO ... and so your main interest is in finding a supplier of titanium dioxide who has experience of the European market.

TOM HALL ...., ..., but even more important is *Confirms, and*
the question of access to supplies. *expands*

LUIGI FRIGERIO Right, I see. And then, ...

.... you're also interested in finding *Leads in to key points*
a second supplier for the American market ...

Extract 3

LUIGI FRIGERIO We recently purchased a small producer in Ohio so we shall
soon be in a position to service the US market too.

TOM HALL Sorry, ... *Signals that he*
wants to recap

.... those locations again.

.... Italy, Spain, Britain and Ireland. *Leads in to key points*

LUIGI FRIGERIO No, ... *Ireland. Holland.* *Corrects and*
The plant is just outside Rotterdam. *expands*

TOM HALL And you've just bought a plant in Ohio?

LUIGI FRIGERIO .... At present the production of this *Confirms and*
plant is relatively low, but ... *expands*

Check your answers in the key **B1.2**

B2 Interaction summary

When exchanging information, it is helpful to check you have understood by *recapping* on key points which the other side has made. This reduces the risk of misunderstandings later in the negotiation.

• A typical sequence for recapping is shown below.

Signal

Perhaps I could just recap on your main points.
I'd just like to go over | *those locations.*
| *your main points.*

Lead in   Key points

As I understand it,	**+**	*H M Griggs is planning an expansion.*
As I recall, you said		*you're also interested in ...*
You said		*Italy, Spain, Britain and Ireland.*

- The other side can then *confirm* or *correct* your understanding and, if necessary, *expand on* the point.

Confirm

> **That's right, yes,**
> **Yes, that's the situation.**
> **That's correct.**

+

Expand

> but even more important is …
>
> At present the production …

Correct

> **No, not** Ireland. **Holland.**

+

Expand

> The plant is just outside Rotterdam.

Note: When you correct somebody, you stress both the wrong word and the right word.

B3 Tasks

1. You are going to recap on your understanding of the other side's interests.
Follow the example.

a. Example

General interest	expanding into Far Eastern markets
Specific interest	agency for our products in Taiwan
Less important interest	mainland Chinese market

Model version **Perhaps I could just recap on your main points. As I understand it, you're interested in expanding into Far Eastern markets and so it's very important for you to establish an agency in Taiwan. And, as I recall, you're interested in the mainland Chinese market, but that's of lesser importance at the moment.**

(You can hear this model version recorded on tape B3.1.)

b. General interest	establishing a US subsidiary
Specific interest	increase market penetration in US
Less important interest	Canada

Compare your answer with the one recorded on tape **B3.1**

2. Listen to tape B3.2. First you will hear someone recapping on a point you have made. Respond following the written instruction. Then you will hear a model version.
Follow the example.

a. Example

You hear	And, as I recall, you're interested in the Korean market, but that's of lesser importance to you.
Instruction	Correct (mainland *Chinese* market) and expand (but not for four or five years).
You	....
Model version	**No, not the Korean market. The mainland Chinese market, but not for four or five years.**

b. Instruction   Confirm and expand. (big potential market)
c. Instruction   Confirm and expand. (also experience of bad weather conditions)
d. Instruction   Correct (adapt existing products) and expand (only small modifications needed).

3. You work for a European company which produces components for the car industry. You are talking to a potential customer. His part of the conversation is on the tape.

Listen to tape B3.3 and follow the interaction plan as you play the role of the potential supplier.

The potential customer starts

Opening statements	– company acquisitions – need for new suppliers.	**YOU**

Recap.

Confirms and expands.

Now listen to the complete interaction on tape B3.4.

C Style – How to be clear and maintain cooperation

CI Focus

1. Listen to tape CI. You will hear five short extracts from the dialogues that you listened to earlier in the unit. After each extract, stop the tape and compare the recorded version with the version in column A below. Write down the words used on tape which correspond to the words in *italics* below.

Follow the example.

A	B Taped version
a. *It's possible that we might be interested* in increasing our options for supply of titanium dioxide.	We're interested in …
b. *We think that it would probably be a good idea to work* with a supplier who has experience and a presence in the European market.	
c. Our domestic market, here in the US, is also expanding and for this market *there's a chance that we might be looking for a second supplier.*	
d. *We assume that you would like to help us.* Maybe at this stage you could …	
e. Good, well *working together could, I'm sure, be beneficial to both our companies.* As you probably know, …	

Check your answers in the key **CI.I**

2. Now put a tick (✓) in one (or more) of the boxes below.

The versions recorded on tape CI are:

a. clearer ☐
b. less clear ☐ than the versions in column A in CI.I.
c. more cooperative ☐

Compare your ideas with those in the key CI.2 **CI.2**

C2 Style summary

- Opening statements should be clear and unambiguous. This will allow the other party to understand your needs and interests. If you express your opening statement too indirectly, it makes it difficult for the other party to know what you really want.

It's possible that we might be interested in increasing ... →	*We're interested in increasing ...*
We think that it would probably be a good idea to ... →	*We'd like to ...*
There's a chance that we might be looking for ... →	*We're also interested in ...*

- Opening statements should also be *independent.* If you make assumptions about the other side's interests, this may irritate them and detract from the climate of cooperation.

We assume that you would like to help us. →	*We think that you are the right kind of company to discuss these needs with.*
Working together could, I'm sure, be beneficial to both our companies. →	*I think we should be able to help you.*

C3 Task

Rewrite the following dialogue so that the statements are clear and unambiguous, and no assumptions are made about the other side's interests.

A: We're aware that the style of advertising in France is very different to that in the UK. So we think that it would probably be a good idea to employ a French agency to design our ads for the French market. We assume that you would like to help us. There's a chance that we might also need advice on special promotional offers, but that's a lower priority at present.

B: Well, we have run several major advertising campaigns for French breweries. I'm sure that working together could be beneficial to both our companies.

Compare your version with the one in the key C3

D Cross-cultural differences – What's going wrong?

DI Focus

Listen to tape D1. You will hear a short extract from a meeting between a German business woman and a British business woman. The German is a buyer for a large chain of department stores and is interested in purchasing clothes manufactured by the British company.

a. What goes wrong?

b. Why does it go wrong?

Now read the comments in the summary below.

D2 Cross-cultural summary

Individuals can have different negotiating styles and differ in the emphasis placed on particular stages of the negotiation. There are cultural differences too.

In the extract you have just heard, the German buyer moves directly from the relationship building phase to the bidding phase without agreeing procedure or exchanging information. While this is a rather extreme example, German negotiators often move to the bidding phase sooner than may be expected by the other side.

Answer key

A Language
••••••••••••••••••••••••••••••••••••

A1.1

a. False   b. True   c. True   d. True   e. False   f. False

A1   🔊

HALL: Well now that we've agreed on the overall procedure for today's meeting, I guess we should move on to the first item on the agenda. Basically, I'd like to tell you our position. But before I do that, I think it would be useful if I gave some very brief background to our company.

FRIGERIO: Yes, that would be helpful.

HALL: Well, H M Griggs **was founded** in 1922. We **manufacture** high quality decorative and industrial paints. **Currently**, we are the fifth largest US paint producer with an **annual turnover** of over $5 billion. In 1982, we started an export division and exports **now account for** 20 per cent of our turnover. This represents an increase of five per cent over the last two years. Over the next five years, we project an even greater increase in our export business. In order to achieve this growth, we are planning a number of key acquisitions in Europe.

So that gives a very rough picture of Griggs – where it's come from, where it's going. Any questions?

FRIGERIO: No, that's very clear.

HALL: Good. Moving on then to the more immediate reason for our meeting today, **we're interested in** increasing our options for supply of titanium dioxide. At the moment we have one main supplier – a US company. We have no complaints about the quality of their products or service, and intend to continue to use this company. However, in line with our export expansion and foreign acquisition plans, especially in Europe, we'd like to work with a supplier who has experience and a presence in the European market. **Our key interest** here is easy access to supplies. This is **extremely important** to us. Our domestic market, here in the US, is also expanding, and for this market we are also interested in looking for a second supplier but at the moment this is **of lesser importance** to us.

We think that you are the right kind of company to discuss these needs with. Maybe at this stage you could tell me a bit more about Italchimica.

A1.2

See tapescript A1 above. The missing words are in **bold**.

A3.1   🔊   Model version

The company was set up by Robert Duval in 1851 in Paris. Currently, Duval S.A. is a world leader in electrical and electronic engineering. We supply telecommunications networks, information systems and electrical installation. We also produce components. We have factories in 15 countries worldwide and employ a total of 200,000 people. Our annual turnover is around $20 billion.

A3.2   🔊   Model version

a. (Example) We're interested in expanding into Far Eastern markets. Our key interest here is to set up an agency for our products in Taiwan. We'd also like to explore the mainland Chinese market, but this is a lower priority.

b. We'd like to establish a US subsidiary. Our key interest here is to increase our market penetration in the US. We're also interested in Canada as a market, but this is of lesser importance at present.

c. We'd like to work with a supplier with experience of offshore platforms. It's imperative for us to find one who has North Sea experience. We're also interested in one who is familiar with advanced design techniques, but that's a lower priority.

d. We're interested in diversifying our activities. Our key interest here is to develop services with higher added value. We'd also like to adapt our products for the international market, but this is a lower priority.

B Interaction

B1.1

i. c ii. Probably.

B1 📼

HALL: Maybe at this stage you could tell me a bit more about Italchimica.

FRIGERIO: Sure. **Perhaps I could just** recap on your main points first, and then I can tell you how I think Italchimica might be able to help you.

HALL: Fine – good idea.

FRIGERIO: So, **as I understand it**, H M Griggs is planning an expansion into Europe, partly through acquisitions …

HALL: That's right, yeah.

FRIGERIO: … and so your main interest is in finding a supplier of titanium dioxide who has experience of the European market.

HALL: **Experience, yes**, but even more important is the question of access to supplies.

FRIGERIO: Right, I see. And then, **as I recall, you said** you're also interested in finding a second supplier for the American market, but that is of lesser importance as you already have an American supplier with whom you are quite satisfied.

HALL: Yeah, that's the situation.

FRIGERIO: Good, well I think we should be able to help you. As you probably know, we're one of the largest producers of titanium dioxide in Europe. We're also the most geographically diverse, with plants in the UK, Holland and Spain, as well as Italy. We recently purchased a small producer in Ohio so we shall soon be in a position to service the US market too.

HALL: Sorry, **I'd just like to go over** those locations again. **You said** Italy, Spain, Britain and Ireland.

FRIGERIO: No, **not** *Ireland. Holland.* The plant is just outside Rotterdam.

HALL: Ah, right. And you've just bought a plant in Ohio?

FRIGERIO: **That's correct**. At present the production of this plant is relatively low, but we have plans for major investment and expansion.

HALL: I see. Well, this seems very …

B1.2

See tapescript B1 above. The missing words are in **bold**.

B3.1 📼 Model version

a. (Example) Perhaps I could just recap on your main points. As I understand it, you're interested in expanding into Far Eastern markets and so it's very important for you to establish an agency in Taiwan. And, as I recall, you're interested in the mainland Chinese market, but that's of lesser importance at the moment.

b. I'd just like to go over your main points. As I understand it, you're interested in establishing a US subsidiary in order to increase market penetration in the US. And you said Canada was also a potential market, but that this is of lesser importance at present.

B3.2 📼

a. (Example)
Speaker: And, as I recall, you're interested in the Korean market, but that's of lesser importance to you.
You: ....
Model version: **No, not the *Korean* market. The mainland *Chinese* market, but not for four or five years.**

b. Speaker: As I recall, you'd also like to get into the Canadian market.
You: ....
Model version: **That's right, yes. We think there's a big potential market there.**

c. Speaker: And as I understand it, you'd prefer a supplier with North Sea experience.
You: ....
Model version: **Yes, that's the situation. We're also interested in a supplier with experience of bad weather conditions.**

d. Speaker: I'd just like to go over some points. You said that you wanted to develop new products for the international market.
You: ....
Model version: **No, not *develop new* products. *Adapt existing* products. Only small modifications would be needed.**

B3.3 📼

CUSTOMER: We've recently acquired two factories in Spain and Portugal, and these, together with our existing plants, give us a good base for further market expansion. We're interested in talking to suppliers who have the capacity to support and service us in these areas.

YOU: ....

CUSTOMER: That's right, and what's more, it must be a supplier with a sufficiently diversified product range.

B3.4 ▭ Complete interaction

CUSTOMER: We've recently acquired two factories in Spain and Portugal, and these, together with our existing plants, give us a good base for further market expansion. We're interested in talking to suppliers who have the capacity to support and service us in these areas.

SUPPLIER: **So, as I understand it, you're looking for a company which would be able to supply you in Spain and Portugal.**

CUSTOMER: That's right, and what's more, it must be a supplier with a sufficiently diversified product range.

C Style

CI ▭

Extract 1

HALL: ... we're interested in increasing our options for supply of titanium dioxide.

Extract 2

HALL: ... we'd like to work with a supplier who has experience and a presence in the European market.

Extract 3

HALL: Our domestic market, here in the US, is also expanding, and for this market we're also interested in looking for a second supplier ...

Extract 4

HALL: We think that you are the right kind of company to discuss these needs with. Maybe at this stage you could ...

Extract 5

FRIGERIO: Good, well I think we should be able to help you. As you probably know ...

CI.I

b. We'd like to work with ...

c. We're also interested in looking for a second supplier.

d. We think that you are the right kind of company to discuss these needs with.

e. I think we should be able to help you.

CI.2

a.

C3 Model version

A: We're aware that the style of advertising in France is very different to that in the UK. So we'd like to employ a French agency to design our ads for the French market. We think that you are the right kind of company to discuss these needs with. We're also interested in getting some advice on special promotional offers, but that's a lower priority at present.

B: Well, we have run several major advertising campaigns for French breweries. So I think that we should be able to help you.

D Cross-cultural differences

DI ▭

ARNDT: ... good I'll take your advice and try that restaurant this evening. On my last few visits to England I've been very impressed by the general standard of restaurants, not at all like the bad image many people in Germany have of English cooking.

BROWN: I'm very pleased to hear that. There have been, I think, big improvements in recent years. Anyway, shall we get down to business ...

ARNDT: Yes, good. My position is that I'm prepared to offer you an item price of £85 for your spring range dresses – up to orders of 2,000 we would expect a discount of at least 5 per cent.

BROWN: I wonder if we could go back a couple of steps and talk about what we hope to achieve in this session.

ARNDT: I'm afraid I don't quite follow you ...

UNIT 4
Questioning

A	Language	How to establish customer needs
B	Interaction	How to deal with questions
C	Style	How to be clear and maintain cooperation
D	Cross-cultural differences	What are the differences?

Background

This is a continuation of the scenario in Unit 3. It is a later part of the same meeting between Luigi Frigerio of Italchimica S.p.A and Tom Hall of H M Griggs Inc.

A Language – How to establish customer needs

A1 Focus

After the opening statements have been made, the supplier will often ask questions to get more information about the customer's needs.

Listen to tape A1. You will now hear a later part of the meeting between Luigi Frigerio and Tom Hall.

1. Decide if the following statements are *true* or *false*.
   a. Luigi Frigerio wants to know exactly how much titanium dioxide Tom Hall orders in a year.
   b. The most important factors for Tom Hall in choosing a supplier are speed of delivery and quality of product.
   c. The environmental issue is not at all important to Tom Hall.
   d. Italchimica's product is more expensive than their competitors'.

   Check your answers in the key **A1.1**

2. Listen to tape A1 again and complete the missing words in the extracts. Then read the notes on the right.

Extract 1

Notes

LUIGI FRIGERIO ....
a few questions about your purchasing policy?

Leads in to the fact that he wants to ask questions

TOM HALL Sure, go ahead.

LUIGI FRIGERIO Well, first of all, ...

titanium dioxide .... normally

.... in a year?

Asks about approximate quantity

Extract 2

LUIGI FRIGERIO I see. You said before that easy access to supplies is extremely important to you.

.... you need a supplier who can deliver at short notice?

Checks an assumption he's made

TOM HALL That's absolutely right. And we really need access to supplies during shortages as well.

LUIGI FRIGERIO Of course. During periods of shortage we supply regular

customers as a matter of priority. ....

.... to another question?

Leads in to a question

.... the

Asks the question

environmental issue .... ?

Extract 3

LUIGI FRIGERIO … Our prices reflect the level of this investment and the high quality of our product.

TOM HALL .... your prices reflect the

Checks an assumption

the investment, ...
that your prices are above current market rates?

LUIGI FRIGERIO Only slightly.

TOM HALL So what can you offer us, Luigi?

LUIGI FRIGERIO That would depend on several factors. ....

Asks about approximate quantity

....
what quantity you might be interested in buying from us?

Check your answers in the key **A1.2**

A2 Language summary

The supplier will often ask questions at this stage to get more information about the customer's needs and the emphasis placed on different factors.

Leading in to questions

| **Can I just ask you** | *a few questions about your purchasing policy?*
about your basic requirements? |

Can I just move on to another question?

Asking for approximate information

| **Roughly** | *how much do you order in a year?*
how many deliveries do you have in a year? |

| **Can you give me an idea of** | *what quantity you might be interested in?*
how many items you might want each month? |

Asking about emphasis

How important is *the environmental issue to you?*
What emphasis do you place on *after-sales service?*

Checking assumptions

Does that mean ...?

| **When you say** | *your prices reflect the investment,*
your production process is clean, | **do you mean that ...?** |

A3 Tasks

1. The questions and expressions below come from a negotiation between a supermarket chain and a coffee supplier. Match the 'questions and expressions' with the 'purposes' on the right.

Follow the example.

Questions/Expressions	Purpose
a. Roughly how much coffee do you buy per year?	i. Leading in to questions
b. When you say a number of suppliers, do you mean a fixed number of regular suppliers?	ii. Asking for approximate information
c. Can I just move on to another question?	iii. Asking about emphasis
d. Roughly what percentage of your annual requirement is for premium coffee?	iv. Checking assumptions
e. Can I just ask you about your buying policy?	
f. What emphasis do you place on quality in relation to price?	

Check your answers in the key **A3.1**

2. You sell training courses in negotiation skills to multinational companies. You are talking to a potential client.

Look at the notes below and follow the instructions on tape A3.2. You will hear five instructions. After each instruction you will hear a model response.

Follow the example.

> *Training requirements* — number of people/year?
> — how many participants/course?
>
> *Training location* — important?

Example

Instruction 1	Lead in to your first area of questioning.
You	....
Model version	**Can I just ask you a few questions about your training requirements?**

B Interaction – How to deal with questions

B1 Focus

When answering questions about your needs, you can either
- give a factual answer

or
- avoid committing yourself.

Now listen to tape B1 (it is the same dialogue as in Section A of this unit).

1. Answer the following questions. Put a tick (✔) in one column.

	Factual	Non-committal
a. Luigi Frigerio asks Tom Hall about quantities. Hall's answer is:		
b. Luigi Frigerio asks Tom Hall about the environmental issue. Hall's answer is:		
c. Tom Hall asks what Luigi Frigerio can offer. Frigerio's answer is:		
d. Luigi Frigerio asks Tom Hall about quantities again. Hall's answer is:		

Check your answers in the key **B1.1**

2. Listen to tape B1 again and complete the missing words in the extracts. Then read the notes on the right.
(**Note:** In these extracts you will be focussing on different aspects of the dialogue from those in Section A1.2.)

Extract 1   *Notes*

LUIGI FRIGERIO Well, first of all, roughly how much titanium dioxide do you normally order in a year?

TOM HALL ....   *Gives factual answer*

– that's overall. So, ... for the export market at present. Probably more next year.

Extract 2

LUIGI FRIGERIO Can I just move on to another question? How important is the environmental issue to you?

TOM HALL Well, ...

manufacturers ....

.... these days.

Gives non-committal answer

Extract 3

TOM HALL So, what can you offer us, Luigi?

LUIGI FRIGERIO ....

....

Gives non-committal answer

Can you give me an idea of what quantity you might be interested in buying from us?

TOM HALL .... , ...

the export market and ....
per cent of our requirements for the US market.

So ....

Gives factual answer

LUIGI FRIGERIO Well, in that case …

Check your answers in the key **B1.2**

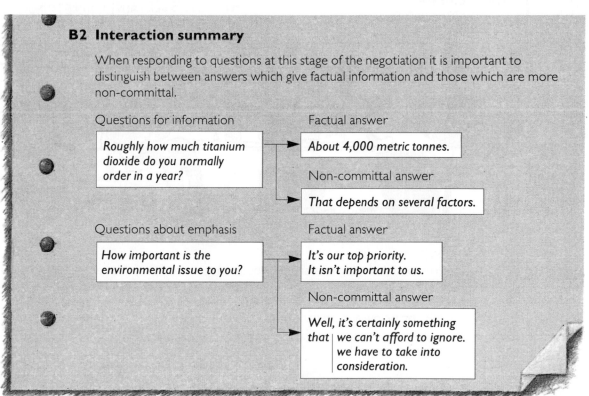

B2 Interaction summary

When responding to questions at this stage of the negotiation it is important to distinguish between answers which give factual information and those which are more non-committal.

Questions for information

> *Roughly how much titanium dioxide do you normally order in a year?*

Factual answer

> *About 4,000 metric tonnes.*

Non-committal answer

> *That depends on several factors.*

Questions about emphasis

> *How important is the environmental issue to you?*

Factual answer

> *It's our top priority.*
> *It isn't important to us.*

Non-committal answer

> *Well, it's certainly something that | we can't afford to ignore.*
> *we have to take into consideration.*

B3 Tasks

1. These are ten exchanges from the negotiation between the supermarket chain and the coffee supplier. Put them in the correct order.

Follow the example.

Phrases from the negotiation

a. Can I just move on to another question? What emphasis do you place on quality in relation to price?

b. Around 1,000 tonnes in total from a number of suppliers.

c. Roughly what percentage of your annual requirement is for premium coffee?

d. Yes, of course.

e. I see. When you say a number of suppliers, do you mean a fixed number of regular suppliers?

f. It depends on which target group we're aiming at. Quality is our top priority if we're buying for the premium coffee market.

START → g. Can I just ask you about your buying policy?   (1)

h. In the region of 10 per cent.

i. Roughly how much coffee do you buy per year?

j. No, but there are some which we do use regularly.

> Check your answers in the key **B3.1**

2. You are responsible for logistics and distribution in your company. You are having a meeting with a computer expert who is interested in selling you a new data processing system for your warehouses. Her part of the conversation is on the tape. Study the interaction plan below and prepare what you want to say.

🔲 When you are ready, listen to tape B3.2 and play the role of the Distribution Manager.

The computer expert starts

| Asks for information. | → | **YOU** |

Give factual answer: approximately 50,000.

Asks for information. ←

Give non-committal answer: not same for all product lines.

Asks about emphasis. ←

Give non-committal answer.

Now listen to the complete interaction on tape B3.3.

C Style – How to be clear and maintain cooperation

C1 Focus

1. Listen to tape C1. You will hear two extracts from a different version of this stage of the negotiation between Luigi Frigerio and Tom Hall.

   As you listen, answer the questions below.

   a. To what extent do the speakers check their assumptions? (Both extracts)

   b How often do they lead in to questions? (Both extracts)

   c. What is Hall's reaction to Frigerio's question about the environmental issue? (Extract 1)

   d. What is Frigerio's reaction to Hall's comment about price? (Extract 2)

   Compare your ideas with those in the key C1.1

2. Now play tape C1 again and compare the recorded extracts with the original versions written below.

   Compare Extract 1 with this:

FRIGERIO: I see. You said before that easy access to supplies is extremely important to you. Does that mean you need a supplier who can deliver at short notice?

HALL: That's absolutely right. And we really need access to supplies during shortages as well.

FRIGERIO: Of course. During periods of shortage we supply regular customers as a matter of priority. Can I just move on to another question? How important is the environmental issue to you?

Hall: Well, it's certainly something that manufacturers …

Compare Extract 2 with this:

FRIGERIO: Our prices reflect the level of this investment and the high quality of our product.

HALL: When you say your prices reflect the investment, do you mean that your prices are above current market rates?

FRIGERIO: Only slightly.

Now put a tick (✔) in one (or more) of the boxes below.

The versions recorded on tape C1 are:

a. less clear ☐

b. more effective ☐ than the versions above.

c. more irritating ☐

Compare your ideas with those in the key **C1.2**

C2 Style summary

At the questioning stage of the negotiation, certain choices about style can also be made.

- The use of a *lead in* to questions gives listeners time to prepare themselves for what you are going to say. It is not necessary to lead in to every question, but it is a useful technique to use to make it clear when there is a change of topic:

… we supply regular customers as a matter of priority. How important is the environmental issue to you? →	*… we supply regular customers as a matter of priority.* **Can I just move on to another question?** *How important is … ?*

- Making assumptions about things said by the other side can be very irritating. In most cases, it will be easier to maintain cooperation by checking that your assumptions are correct.

That means that you need a supplier who can deliver at short notice. →	**Does that mean** *you need a supplier who can deliver at short notice?*
In other words, your product is very expensive. →	**When you say** *your prices reflect the investment,* **do you mean that** *your prices are above current market rates?*

C3 Task

Listen to tape C3. You will hear four exchanges between two speakers. In each exchange, the second speaker makes an assumption. Rephrase what the second speaker says, so that you *check* the assumption. You will then hear a model version.

Follow the example.

Example

Speaker A	We have 20 warehouses.
Speaker B	In other words, you have warehouses all over the country.
You	....
Model version	**Does that mean you have warehouses all over the country?**

D Cross-cultural differences – What are the differences?

DI Focus

Below are two advertisements, one for an American airline, the other for a German airline. These advertisements reflect certain cultural orientations.

Read the advertisements then answer the questions below.

LONDON

JUST BECAUSE YOUR SEAT HAS A NUMBER DOESN'T MEAN YOU SHOULD BE TREATED LIKE ONE.

'Use Passenger Names.'

This reminder appears on virtually every page of the Delta Air Lines Stewardess Training Manual.

We believe a cup of coffee leaves a nicer taste in your client's mouth when it's given to them by name.

It's just one of the personal touches we encourage from everyone at Delta, from the ground staff to the Captain in command of your client's flight.

Of course, caring and consideration can't be taught. It's something you either have or you haven't.

We think it helps that our home is Atlanta. People from the South tend to have a lot of outmoded ideas about service.

They haven't yet learnt how to fake a smile. They haven't cultivated the attitude that by serving you they're doing you a favour.

But don't take our word for it. Any airline can claim service. At Delta we have the facts to support it.

Delta has been number one in passenger satisfaction among major US airlines for the past 15 years.*

However, in-flight service and experience don't count for much if the plane isn't going where your clients want to be.

Delta has non-stop flights each day from London Gatwick to Cincinnati and Atlanta. Our US gateways are so convenient your clients will literally fly through customs and immigration.

So now we'd like to treat you to a number.

Our reservation line is on 0800 414 767.

CINCINNATI

ATLANTA

DELTA AIR LINES
We Love To Fly And It Shows.

*Based on consumer complaint statistics compiled by the US Department of Transportation. ©1990 Delta Air Lines, Inc.

Before we buy a new plane, we improve it. Lufthansa.

Many people feel that the term "German engineering", and the perfection that goes with it, is somewhat overstated. But that is one accusation we've always been happy to accept when it comes to our aircraft and your peace of mind. Because that's an area where we refuse to overlook even the slightest detail. Take, for instance, the new Boeing 747-400. We've invested more than 20,000 engineering hours in it. A long list of fundamental features, such as the cockpit concept, can be traced back to our recommendations. And altogether over 400 detailed improvements are the result of our close cooperation with the manufacturer. But even that isn't enough: on the new 747-400, our technical teams carried out over 1,000 additional checks on top of the manufacturer's own quality control.

There's probably no other airline in the world which inspects and controls its technology, its equipment and its aircraft systems more meticulously than Lufthansa. For example, Lufthansa was the world's first airline to practise a radical and far-sighted technology that checks the health of our engines every second they're in flight. And every new piece of knowledge is immediately translated into new improvements, which add up to our philosophy of uncompromising quality and perfection.

Perhaps we really are too exacting, but we believe we owe that to you and our good name.

Lufthansa

a. What is the basic difference in advertising approach?

b. What are the implications of this difference for the questioning stage of a negotiation?

Compare your ideas with those in the key **DI**

D2 Cross-cultural summary

Different national cultures place different emphases on the main selling features of a product or service.

The advertisement for the American airline, Delta Airlines, which was designed for a British target audience, stresses personal service and benefits to the customer. The advertisement for Lufthansa, the German airline, talks about technical features and exemplifies these features by quoting relevant facts.

Clearly, when preparing for an international negotiation, it is important to take into account differences of this kind. This is particularly important when working out the focus of questions to establish customer needs. An American or British buyer may expect lots of questions from the seller before any presentation of benefits is made. A German buyer may expect a clear and factual presentation of technical features supported by concrete examples but relatively few questions about needs.

Answer key

A Language

A1.1

a. False   b. False   c. False   d. True

A1 📼

FRIGERIO: **Can I just ask you** a few questions about your purchasing policy?

HALL: Sure, go ahead.

FRIGERIO: Well, first of all, **roughly how much** titanium dioxide **do you** normally **order** in a year?

HALL: About 4,000 metric tonnes – that's overall. So, around 800 tonnes for the export market at present. Probably more next year.

FRIGERIO: I see. You said before that easy access to supplies is extremely important to you. **Does that mean** you need a supplier who can deliver at short notice?

HALL: That's absolutely right. And we really need access to supplies during shortages as well.

FRIGERIO: Of course. During periods of shortage we supply regular customers as a matter of priority. **Can I just move on** to another question? **How important is** the environmental issue **to you**?

HALL: Well, it's certainly something that manufacturers can't afford to ignore these days. What exactly are you getting at, Luigi?

FRIGERIO: Well, as you no doubt remember, there was a big demand for titanium dioxide a couple of years ago; it was a seller's market.

HALL: Sure, how could I forget?

FRIGERIO: At that time Italchimica made a considerable investment in a new 'clean' production process, which doesn't have such an adverse effect on the environment. Our prices reflect the level of this investment and the high quality of our product.

HALL: **When you say** your prices reflect the investment, **do you mean** that your prices are above current market rates?

FRIGERIO: Only slightly.

HALL: So what can you offer us, Luigi?

FRIGERIO: That would depend on several factors. **Can you give me an idea of** what quantity you might be interested in buying from us?

HALL: Initially, the 800 tonnes for the export market, and up to 20 per cent of our requirements for the US market. So about 1,400 tonnes.

FRIGERIO: Well, in that …

A1.2

See tapescript A1 above. The missing words are in **bold**.

A3.1

a. ii   b. iv   c. i   d. ii   e. i   f. iii

A3.2 📼

(Example) Instruction 1: Lead in to your first area of questioning.

You: ....

Model version: **Can I just ask you a few questions about your training requirements?**

Instruction 2: Ask for approximate information about the number of people.

You: ....

Model version: **Roughly how many people do you want to train per year?**

Instruction 3: Ask for approximate information about the number of participants on each course.

You: ....

Model version: **Can you give me an idea of how many participants you would have on each course?**

Instruction 4: Lead in to your next question.

You: ....

Model version: **Can I just move on to another question?**

Instruction 5: Ask about emphasis on training location.

You: ....

Model version: **How important is the training location to you?**

B Interaction

B1 📼

See tapescript A1.

B1.1

a. factual   b. non-committal
c. non-committal d. factual

B1.2

Extract 1

HALL: **About 4,000 metric tonnes** – that's overall. So, **around 800 tonnes** for the export market at present. Probably more next year.

Extract 2

HALL: Well, **it's certainly something that** manufacturers **can't afford to ignore** these days.

Extract 3

FRIGERIO: **That would depend on several factors.** Can you give me an idea of what quantity you might be interested in buying from us?

HALL: **Initially, the 800 tonnes for** the export market, and **up to 20** per cent of our requirements for the US market. So **about 1,400 tonnes**.

B3.1

1. g 2. d 3. i 4. b 5. e 6. j 7. a 8. f 9. c 10. h

B3.2 📼

COMPUTER EXPERT: So, you told me before that you've got 20 warehouses. Can you give me an idea of how many items you have in stock at any given time?

YOU: ....

COMPUTER EXPERT: And is that distributed evenly over the entire country?

YOU: ....

COMPUTER EXPERT: I see. And another thing. How important is system security to you?

YOU: ....

B3.3 📼 Complete interaction

COMPUTER EXPERT: So, you told me before that you've got 20 warehouses. Can you give me an idea of how many items you have in stock at any given time?

DISTRIBUTION MANAGER: **Yes, about 50,000 items.**

COMPUTER EXPERT: And is that distributed evenly over the entire country?

DISTRIBUTION MANAGER: **That depends on the product line.**

COMPUTER EXPERT: I see. And another thing. How important is system security to you?

DISTRIBUTION MANAGER: **Well, it's certainly something that we can't afford to ignore.**

C Style

C1.1

a. Not at all. They make assumptions, but do not check them.

b Never.

c. He doesn't understand it (probably because the change in topic is too sudden).

d. He is defensive.

C1 📼

Extract 1

FRIGERIO: I see. You said before that easy access to supplies is extremely important to you. That means you need a supplier who can deliver at short notice.

HALL: Yes, but that's only one aspect of the matter. We really need access to supplies during shortages as well.

FRIGERIO: Of course. During periods of shortage we supply regular customers as a matter of priority. How important is the environmental issue to you?

HALL: Sorry, I don't quite follow you. What did you say?

Extract 2

FRIGERIO: At that time, Italchimica made a considerable investment in a new 'clean' production process, which doesn't have such an adverse effect on the environment. Our prices reflect the level of this investment and the high quality of our product.

HALL: In other words, your product is very expensive.

FRIGERIO: I wouldn't say that. Our prices are above current market rates, but only slightly.

C1.2

a. and c.

C3 📼

1. Speaker A: We have 20 warehouses.
   Speaker B: In other words, you have warehouses all over the country.
   You: ....

Model version: **Does that mean you have warehouses all over the country?**

2. Speaker A: Our requirements for bottled water fluctuate during the year.

Speaker B: That means you order more during the summer.

You: ....

Model version: **When you say your requirements fluctuate, do you mean that you order more during the summer?**

3. Speaker A: This new product is 100 per cent environmentally friendly.

Speaker B: In other words, your product has absolutely no adverse effects on the environment.

You: ....

Model version: **When you say 100 per cent environmentally friendly, do you mean that your product has absolutely no adverse effects on the environment?**

4. Speaker A: We can offer you this model in a range of neutral colours.

Speaker B: That means black, white and grey, I suppose.

You: ....

Model version: **Does that mean black, white and grey?**

D Cross-cultural differences

D I

a. The advertisement for the German airline emphasises technical reliability. The advertisement for the American airline emphasises personal service.

b. A German buyer may not expect a lot of questioning about his needs, as his decision is more likely to be based on the technical benefits of the product or service.

Options

A *Language*	How to generate options
B *Interaction*	How to evaluate options
C *Style*	How to express personal reactions
D *Cross-cultural differences*	What's the explanation?

Background

Clark-Maxwell is a British management training and consultancy company which is interested in establishing a greater European presence. It is currently in discussion with FCF, a French training organisation in Lyon. The two companies are looking at ways in which they could work more closely together in the French market. They have worked together a little in the past and have met several times recently to discuss closer cooperation.

A Language – How to generate options

A1 Focus

The next essential step in a negotiation is for the two sides to brainstorm a lot of different ideas or options for working together. At this stage it is important not to evaluate or criticise the ideas.

🖭 Listen to tape A1. You will now hear part of a meeting between the French and British negotiating teams.

Taking part in the meeting are

Peter Johnson	Clark-Maxwell
Jane Parsons	Clark-Maxwell
Yves Guillet	FCF
Pascale Lannoy	FCF

1. Decide if the following statements are *true* or *false*.

   a. The two sides have not got enough information about each other's companies yet.

   b. Johnson has already decided on how they could work together.

   c. Licensing their product seems to be a new idea for the British.

   d. They spend a long time talking about agency agreements.

Check your answers in the key **A1.1**

2. Listen to tape A1 again and complete the missing words. Then read the notes on the right.

Extract	*Notes*

YVES GUILLET … before making any decisions.

.... that

       Introduces the idea of generating options

there are ....

.... we could work more closely together.

I suggest we ....

       Introduces the process of generating options

.... and then examine them in more detail one by one.

PASCALE LANNOY Good idea.

YVES GUILLET So, do you want to begin, Pascale?

PASCALE LANNOY Yes, ...

       Puts forward an option

.... that we form a joint company, separate from both our present organisations, but with joint shareholding.

JANE PARSONS .... this new European Economic Interest Grouping, an EEIG, as an umbrella for our activities? This would be cheaper and quicker, and probably less bureaucratic.

       Puts forward an option

YVES GUILLET ....

       Puts forward an option

.... licensing your Total Quality training programme for us to use in France?

PETER JOHNSON I hadn't thought of that.

       Puts forward an option

.... , of course, look at the idea of FCF acting as our agents in France.

PASCALE LANNOY I think if we are considering this route ....

       Puts forward an option

.... franchising.

YVES GUILLET OK. Well, ... go through each of these …

       Makes a suggestion

Check your answers in the key **A1.2**

A2 Language summary

Having exchanged information and clarified positions, it is now important for the negotiators to generate ideas or options before making any decisions. This is a creative and imaginative process and can be broken down into the following stages:

Introducing the idea of generating options

> **It seems to me that there are a number of ways we could** work together.
>
> **There seem to be several possibilities for** working more closely together.

Introducing the process of generating options

> **Shall/ I suggest** | **we list the options first and then examine them in more detail one by one?**
>
> **Should we brainstorm the options before we discuss any in detail?**

Putting forward options

> **I'd like to start by suggesting ...**
>
> **How about** | **trying ... ?**
> | **using ... ?**
>
> **Have you considered the idea of ... ?**
> **We could also ...**

Suggesting a move to the next stage in the process

> **Why don't we go through each of these in more detail.**
>
> **At this stage I think we should look at each option in turn.**

A3 Task

The management team of a sports goods manufacturer is meeting to discuss ways to deal with the problem of poor sales, a shrinking market and rising costs.

Listen to tape A3. You will hear six instructions asking you to generate options in the context of that discussion. You will then hear a model version.

Follow the example.

Example

Instruction 1   You want to introduce the idea of generating options.

You   ....

Model version **It seems to me that there are a number of ways we could solve our problems.**
                or
                There seem to be several possibilities for dealing with this.

B Interaction – How to evaluate options

B1 Focus

After generating a number of options, the next step is to evaluate each one, giving reasons for and against, and your reactions to other people's ideas.

Listen to tape B1. You will hear a second extract from the same meeting.

1. The two sides are now evaluating the options. Mark the options A (attractive), U (unattractive) or N (no comment given) in the same way as they are evaluated by the two sides.

	French	British
a. Franchising		
b. Licensing		
c. Forming an EEIG		
d. Forming a joint company		

Check your answers in the key **B1.1**

2. Listen to tape B1 again and complete the missing words in the extracts. Then read the notes on the right.

Extract 1   *Notes*

YVES GUILLET   Well, ... the ....   *Gives reason for his evaluation*

.... of this for us is that we would simply be acting as

a vehicle for your products and services. There would be very

little real joint activity. So .... that was the   *Evaluates this option*

....

JANE PARSONS   .... Yves.   *Reacts to Yves's evaluation*
Perhaps we should discount that option.

Extract 2

PASCALE LANNOY ... our philosophy about meeting client needs. ....

Gives reason for her evaluation

....
licensing is that the French market has very particular needs
and you can't just transfer a programme that works well in
the UK and expect it to work here too.

So ....

Evaluates this option

licensing as a fairly .... as well.

JANE PARSONS .... , ... that ....

Reacts to Pascale's evaluation

.... with the way we look at the situation too.
How about the idea of forming an EEIG?

PETER JOHNSON I think that's ....

Evaluates this option

....

The main .... of an EEIG, as ....

Gives reason for his evaluation

.... , is that it will give us the opportunity
to work closely together, but with maximum flexibility.

YVES GUILLET .... We're also interested in close cooperation,

Reacts to Peter's evaluation

.... I feel ...

Check your answers in the key `B1.2`

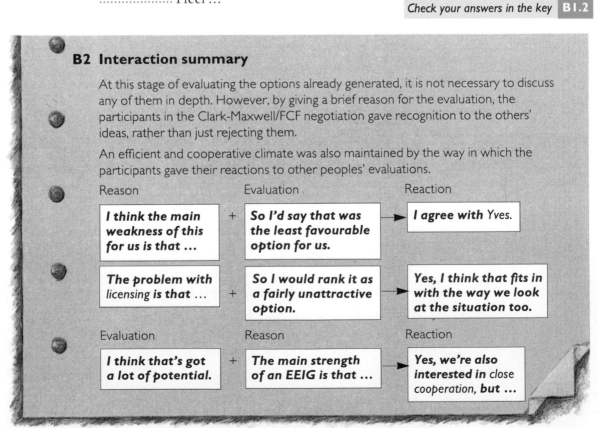

B2 Interaction summary

At this stage of evaluating the options already generated, it is not necessary to discuss
any of them in depth. However, by giving a brief reason for the evaluation, the
participants in the Clark-Maxwell/FCF negotiation gave recognition to the others'
ideas, rather than just rejecting them.

An efficient and cooperative climate was also maintained by the way in which the
participants gave their reactions to other peoples' evaluations.

Reason	Evaluation	Reaction
I think the main weakness of this for us is that ... +	**So I'd say that was the least favourable option for us.** →	**I agree with** Yves.
The problem with licensing **is that ...** +	**So I would rank it as a fairly unattractive option.** →	**Yes, I think that fits in with the way we look at the situation too.**

Evaluation	Reason	Reaction
I think that's got a lot of potential. +	**The main strength of an EEIG is that ...** →	**Yes, we're also interested in** close cooperation, **but ...**

B3 Tasks

1. The expressions below come from a discussion about how to fill a key vacancy in a company. Match the expressions with the purposes on the right. Follow the example.

Expressions	Purpose
a. The main weakness of that approach is that it's a time-consuming process.	i. giving an evaluation
b. I think that idea's got a lot of potential.	ii. giving a reason
c. I'd rank that as the least favourable option.	iii. reacting
d. Yes, I think that fits in with how I look at the situation too.	
e. Yes, it's a lengthy process, but it does give us access to a wide range of candidates.	
f. So, I'd say that was an unattractive option.	
g. The main strength of it is that the candidate will know our products and company culture.	
h. The problem with headhunters is that they're very expensive and they don't always find the right sort of candidate.	

Check your answers in the key **B3.1**

2. Now use the expressions from B3.1 to complete this discussion about filling a key vacancy. Use the notes on the right to help you. Follow the example.

Notes

ANN: So what about the idea of using a headhunter?

i. BOB: The problem with headhunters is that they're very expensive and they don't always find the right sort of candidate. — *Gives reason*

ii. .... *Gives evaluation*

CATHY: I agree. So what about advertising?

iii. ANN: .... *Gives reason*

iv. .... *Gives evaluation*

v. BOB: .... *Reacts*

CATHY: OK. We'll come back to that option later. What about the third idea – internal promotion?

vi. ANN: .... *Gives evaluation*

vii. .... *Gives reason*

viii. CATHY: .... *Reacts*

Check your answers in the key **B3.2**

C Style – How to express personal reactions

C1 Focus

📼 1. Listen to tape C1. You will hear four short extracts from one of the dialogues you listened to earlier in the unit. After each extract, stop the tape and compare the recorded version with the version in column A below. Write down the words used on tape which do not appear in the versions in column A.

Follow the example.

A	B Taped version
a. It doesn't fit in with our philosophy about meeting client needs.	*Well, my immediate feeling is that…*
b. Yes, that fits in with the way we look at the situation too.	
c. The main strength of an EEIG is that it will give us the opportunity to work closely together …	
d. … but we should go even further than that and seriously consider a joint company.	

Check your answers in the key **C1.1**

2. Now put a tick (✔) in one (or more) of the boxes below.

The versions in column A are:

a. more effective ☐
b. less personal ☐ than those recorded on tape C1.
c. more direct ☐

Compare your ideas with those in the key **C1.2**

C2 Style summary

Research suggests that at this stage of generating and evaluating options, skilled and successful negotiators give a clear indication of their *feelings* about the possibilities. Failure to do this may have a negative influence on the negotiation.

It doesn't fit in with our philosophy. →	**My immediate feeling is** *that it doesn't fit in with our philosophy.*
That fits in with the way we look at it. →	**I think** *that fits in with the way we look at it.*
The main strength of this is that … →	*The main strength of this,* **as we see it,** *is that …*
	The main strength of this, **from our point of view,** *is that …*
We should go even further than that. →	**I feel** *we should go even further than that.*
That's an unusual suggestion. →	**I'm not sure how to react** *to that suggestion.*
Probably that would not be a good option. →	**I have some doubts** *about that option.*

C3 Task

 Listen to tape C3. You will hear four options put forward for dealing with the problems of the sports goods manufacturer. React, following the written instruction. In each case you should give a clear indication of your *feelings*.

Follow the example.

Example

Option 1	I'd like to start by suggesting an intensive sales campaign.
Instruction 1	You think this option would be too expensive.
You	....
Model version	**My immediate feeling is that it would be too expensive.** *or* **I feel that would be too expensive.**

Instruction 2	You think this option is very attractive.
Instruction 3	You don't think this is a good option.
Instruction 4	You think this is the best short-term solution.

D Cross-cultural differences – What's the explanation?

D1 Focus

Read the short case study, then answer the question at the end.

Two representatives of an American toiletries company met managers from an Indonesian import company to discuss a franchising agreement. An agreement to set up an Indonesian franchise operation had already been reached in principle, but when one of the Americans suggested a brainstorming session to generate ideas for the packaging and promotion of the products for the Indonesian market, she was disappointed with the reaction she got.

Present at that stage of the negotiation, on the American side, were Ted Willis, Head of South-East Asian Operations, and Alison Rockwell, International Marketing Manager. The Indonesians were represented by Bambang Sucipto, Managing Director of the import company and Rudi Sutopo, who had been chosen as Marketing and Distribution Manager for the new franchise.

Although Bambang Sucipto contributed some ideas at the brainstorming stage, Rudi Sutopo remained silent, even when specifically asked for his ideas and opinions. In the hotel bar that evening, Alison Rockwell expressed her reservations about the project: 'What's wrong with that guy Rudi? He didn't say a word in the meeting today. I don't know if I can even work with him in the future – he's got no ideas, no dynamism! After all, he's the one who should know the Indonesian market – he can't expect me to supply him with all the ideas!'

Ted Willis, who had much more experience of dealing with Indonesians, offered his interpretation of the situation.

What do you think it was?

Compare your ideas with those in the key **D1**

■ 61

D2 Cross-cultural summary

This case study reflects a number of aspects of cultural difference:

1. Some cultures tend to be *collectivist,* and others *individualist.* In a collectivist culture this means that group harmony generally takes precedence over individual performance and/or needs. Examples of collectivist cultures are Japan, Indonesia, Venezuela and Portugal. Examples of individualist cultures are the United States, Britain and Italy.

2. The distribution of power within companies will also vary from culture to culture. In cultures with a *low power distance*, for example, Sweden and the United States, there is relatively little emphasis on status. In cultures with a *high power distance*, such as Mexico and Indonesia, position and status play a more important role in working relationships. It must be remembered, of course, that within any culture there will be variations in power distance from company to company.

Answer key

A Language

A1.1

a. False   b. True   c. True   d. False

A1 🔊

JOHNSON: Well, I think we've both got a good idea of each other's capabilities and experience. So the next step is to decide on the best way for our companies to work together. I feel that, initially, we should work on an informal partnership basis, to see how things go.

GUILLET: I think it would be better to look at all the possible options first, before making any decisions. **It seems to me** that there are **a number of ways** we could work more closely together. I suggest we **list the options first** and then examine them in more detail one by one.

LANNOY: Good idea.

GUILLET: So, do you want to begin, Pascale?

LANNOY: Yes, **I'd like to start by suggesting** that we form a joint company, separate from both of our present organisations, but with joint shareholding.

PARSONS: **How about using** this new European Economic Interest Grouping, an EEIG, as an umbrella for our activities? This would be cheaper and quicker, and probably less bureaucratic.

GUILLET: **Have you considered the idea of** licensing your Total Quality training programme for us to use in France?

JOHNSON: I hadn't thought of that. **We could also**, of course, look at the idea of FCF acting as our agents in France.

LANNOY: I think if we are considering this route, **we should also look at** franchising.

GUILLET: OK. Well, **why don't we** go through each of these in more detail now. We'll probably find that some of them aren't what we want at all, and we can then concentrate on the best ones.

A1.2

See tapescript A1 above. The missing words are in **bold**.

A3 🔊

(Example) Instruction 1: You want to introduce the idea of generating options.

You: ....

Model version: **It seems to me that there are a number of ways we could solve our problems.**

or

There seem to be several possibilities for dealing with this.

Instruction 2: You want to introduce the process of generating options.

You: ....

Model version: **Shall we list the options first and then examine them in more detail one by one?**

or

Should we brainstorm the options before we discuss any in detail?

Instruction 3: Put forward the option of an intensive sales campaign.

You: ....

Model version: **I'd like to start by suggesting an intensive sales campaign.**

Instruction 4: Put forward the option of diversifying into leisurewear.

You: ....

Model version: **How about diversifying into leisurewear?**

or

We could also diversify into leisurewear.

Instruction 5: Put forward the option of a big reduction in personnel.

You: ....

Model version: **Have you considered the idea of a big reduction in personnel?**

Instruction 6: Suggest moving to the next stage in the process.

You: ....

Model version: **Why don't we now go through each of these options in detail?**

or

At this stage I think we should look at each option in turn.

B Interaction

B1.1

a. French – U	British – U
b. French – U	British – U
c. French – N	British – A
d. French – A	British – N

B1

JOHNSON: Pascale, you mentioned franchising. What do the others think?

GUILLET: Well, **I think** the **main weakness** of this for us is that we would simply be acting as a vehicle for your products and services. There would be very little real joint activity. So **I'd say** that was the **least favourable option for us**.

PARSONS: **I agree with** Yves. Perhaps we should discount that option. I think we should look for a more synergistic solution – one that will enable us to combine our different experience and capabilities to produce a really good new range of services.

JOHNSON: How about the suggestion of licensing?

LANNOY: Well, my immediate feeling is that it doesn't fit in with our philosophy about meeting client needs. **I feel the problem with** licensing is that the French market has very particular needs and you can't just transfer a programme that works well in the UK and expect it to work here too. So **I would rank** licensing as a fairly **unattractive option** as well.

PARSONS: **Yes, I think** that **fits in** with the way we look at the situation too. How about the idea of forming an EEIG?

JOHNSON: I think that's **got a lot of potential**. The main **strength** of an EEIG, as **we see it**, is that it will give us the opportunity to work closely together, but with maximum flexibility.

GUILLET: **Yes.** We're also interested in close cooperation, **but** I feel we should go even further than that and seriously consider a joint company. I think that …

B1.2

See tapescript B1 above. The missing words are in **bold**.

B3.1

a. ii   b. i   c. i   d. iii   e. iii   f. i   g. ii   h. ii

B3.2

ANN: So what about the idea of using a headhunter?

i. BOB: **The problem with headhunters is that they're very expensive and they don't always find the right sort of candidate.** (h)

ii. **So I'd say that was an unattractive option.** (f)

CATHY: I agree. So what about advertising?

iii. ANN: **The main weakness of that approach is that it's a time-consuming process.** (a)

iv. **I'd rank that as the least favourable option.** (c)

v. BOB: **Yes, it's a lengthy process, but it does give us access to a wide range of candidates.** (e)

CATHY: OK. We'll come back to that option later.

What about the third idea – internal promotion?

vi. ANN: **I think that idea's got a lot of potential.** (b)

vii. **The main strength of it is that the candidate will know our products and company culture.** (g)

viii. CATHY: **Yes, I think that fits in with how I look at the situation too.** (d)

C Style

C1.1

b. Yes, **I think** that fits in with …

c. The main strength of an EEIG, **as we see it**, is …

d. but **I feel** we should go even further …

C1

Extract 1

LANNOY: Well, my immediate feeling is that it doesn't fit in with our philosophy about meeting client needs.

Extract 2

PARSONS: Yes, I think that fits in with the way we look at the situation too.

Extract 3

JOHNSON: The main strength of an EEIG, as we see it, is that it will give us the opportunity to work closely together ..

Extract 4

GUILLET: … but I feel we should go even further than that and seriously consider a joint company.

C1.2

b.

C3 📼

Option 1: I'd like to start by suggesting an intensive sales campaign.

You: ....

Model version: **My immediate feeling is that it would be too expensive.**

or

I feel that would be too expensive.

Option 2: How about diversifying into leisurewear?

You: ....

Model version: **From my point of view that's a very attractive option.**

Option 3: Have you considered the idea of a big reduction in personnel?

You: ....

Model version: **I have some doubts about that option.**

Option 4: We could also stop production of our less profitable lines.

You: ....

Model version: **As I see it, this is the best short-term solution.**

or

I think this is the best short-term solution.

D Cross-cultural differences
· ·

D1

The most probable explanation is that Rudi Sutopo, as a newly-appointed manager, does not want to disturb the harmony of his relationship with Bambang Sucipto by appearing pushy. In Indonesia, senior members of a negotiating team are deferred to because of their rank and status. In the United States, members of a negotiating team are expected to contribute on an individual basis. There is a further possibility that Rudi Sutopo would not wish to lose face by offering suggestions which might not tie in with Bambang Sucipto's overall strategy. Possibly this process of generating options would be unfamiliar to him, as it is a very Western approach. In some Asian countries, as well as in the Middle East, sending a woman to do business might lead to cross-cultural problems. However, in Indonesia this is unlikely to be the case. Although the majority of the population is Islamic, it is a secular society and women are accepted in business.

Bidding

A	*Language*	How to put forward reasons and proposals
B	*Interaction*	How to clarify and react to proposals
C	*Style*	How to maintain a climate of cooperation
D	*Cross-cultural differences*	What's the explanation?

Background

This is a continuation of the scenario in Unit 5, in which Clark-Maxwell and the French company, FCF, are exploring ways of working more closely together. It is two days later. The decision to set up a joint company has been taken and agreement has been reached on a number of specific issues. This unit covers the early part of the discussion about the name for the new company, in which each side puts forward their proposals.

A Language – How to put forward reasons and proposals

A1 Focus

The heart of a negotiation is the bidding phase, when the two parties put forward proposals and bids.

Listen to tape A1. You will now hear part of the meeting between members of the French and British negotiating teams.

1. Decide if the following statements are *true* or *false*.

   a. Jane Parsons does not give a clear reason for wanting to use the name Clark-Maxwell.
   b. The two sides put different emphasis on the relative importance of multinational clients for the new company.
   c. The French do not make a clear proposal.
   d. The third proposal is a compromise.

Check your answers in the key **A1.1**

2. Listen to tape A1 again and complete the missing words in the extracts. Then read the notes on the right.

Extract 1

Notes

JANE PARSONS … As you know, we have an established reputation in the UK, and last year we also set up companies in Germany and Italy. Many of our clients are multinational companies and, in all three countries, they're used to doing business with us under

the name Clark-Maxwell. .... , ...

Puts forward a reason

Makes a proposal

.... the new company in France .... also have the name Clark-Maxwell.

Extract 2

YVES GUILLET … We feel that the biggest potential in France for the products and services of the new company is among medium-sized French companies. Many of these companies will never have heard the name Clark-Maxwell. It will mean nothing to them, I'm afraid.

Puts forward a reason

JANE PARSONS I see what you mean. Well, that's certainly something we'll have to take into account.

YVES GUILLET And there are a couple of other points. .... , the name

Clark-Maxwell sounds very English, and .... , it says nothing about the type of activity the company is involved in.

Puts forward a reason

....

to create a completely new name which will reflect the identity and role of the new company.

Makes a proposal

Extract 3

PETER JOHNSON … Existing clients of yours, and ours, might not appreciate the experience and know-how that we've brought to this new venture. It might appear to be a completely new and inexperienced firm.

....

Makes a proposal

.... combine both our names.

Check your answers in the key **A1.2**

A2 Language summary

- When putting forward proposals and bids, it is important to do so *clearly* and *firmly*.

  We propose that the new company **should have the name ...**
  Our proposal is to create a completely new name...
  We propose that we combine both names.

- As the discussion develops, it is common for other people to put forward alternative or additional proposals in a more tentative way.

  Maybe a better solution would be to ...
  It could be a good idea to ...
  Alternatively, we could ...

In the extracts you have just listened to, the negotiators first stated their *reasons* for making a proposal, *then* made the proposal. In many cases this is a good strategy, because it lowers the risk of potential objections. If you make the proposal first, the other side will be thinking of objections to it while you are giving your reasons.

Reason	Proposal
... Many of our clients are multi-national companies and they ... are used to doing business with us under the name Clark-Maxwell. **+**	*Therefore, we propose that the new company in France should also have the name Clark-Maxwell.*

A3 Tasks

1. Expand the notes below to produce a reason followed by a proposal.

   Follow the example.

   a. **Example**

Reason	Proposal
Nigerian subsidiary running at a loss for last two years.	Close it down.

   Model version   **The Nigerian subsidiary has been running at a loss for the last two years. Therefore, our proposal is to close it down.**

(You can hear this model version recorded on tape A3.1.)

Reason	Proposal
b. Labour costs in Sweden very high.	Move production to Portugal.
c. Market for personal computers very competitive.	Concentrate on software development.
d. Developing this new refining process cost company a lot of money.	Try to sell it under licence to other companies.
e. Company expanding into international markets.	Invest in language training.

Compare your answers with those recorded on tape   **A3.1**

2. In response to the proposals made above, put forward alternative or additional proposals in a more tentative way.

Follow the example.

a. Example

Original proposal	Other proposal
Our proposal is to close down the Nigerian subsidiary.	Look at ways of making it it more cost-effective.

Model version   **Maybe a better solution would be to look at ways of making it more cost-effective.**

(You can hear this model version recorded on tape A3.2.)

Original proposal	Other proposal
b. So we propose that we should move production to Portugal.	Expand factory in UK.
c. Therefore our proposal is to concentrate on software development.	Diversify into other types of office equipment.
d. Therefore we propose that we should try to sell it under licence to other companies.	Charge a royalty fee too.
e. So, our proposal is to invest more money in language training.	Recruit bilingual staff.

Compare your answers with those recorded on tape **A3.2**

B Interaction – How to clarify and react to proposals

B1 Focus

Before accepting or rejecting a proposal, you will minimise the risk of confusion or misunderstandings if you:

- clarify your understanding of what the other side is proposing.
- give a clear reaction to the other side's reasons and proposals.

Now listen to tape B1 (it is the same dialogue as in Section A of this unit).

1. Answer the following questions.
    i. Clark-Maxwell feel that their name has a clear identity for multinational clients. Do FCF:
        a. accept this argument?
        b. understand this argument?
        c. reject this argument completely?
    ii. FCF feel that the name Clark-Maxwell will be unknown to many French companies. Do Clark-Maxwell:
        a. accept this argument?
        b. understand this argument?
        c. reject this argument completely?
    iii. FCF propose creating a completely new name. Is Clark-Maxwell's first reaction:
        a. to accept this proposal?
        b. to reject this proposal?
        c. to ask for more details of the proposal?

Check your answers in the key **B1.1**

2. Rewind the cassette and listen to tape B1 again. Complete the missing words in the extracts. Then read the notes on the right.

(**Note:** In these extracts you will be focussing on different aspects of the dialogue from those in Section A1.2.)

Extract 1

Notes

JANE PARSONS Therefore, we propose that the new company in France should also have the name Clark-Maxwell.

Makes a proposal

PASCALE LANNOY I see. So, ...

.... , you feel that using the name Clark-Maxwell in France too will give the new company a clear identity in the eyes of multinational clients?

Asks for clarification of Clark-Maxwell's interests

PETER JOHNSON ....

And what's more, our best-known training package, the Total Quality Management Programme, is associated with our name.

Confirms Pascale's understanding. Adds another reason

YVES GUILLET Oh, ... Of course multinational clients are very important.

Reacts to Clark-Maxwell's reason

.... , we shouldn't forget that one of our objectives in forming this new company is to enter new markets.

Extract 2

YVES GUILLET Many of these companies will never have heard the name Clark-Maxwell. It will mean nothing to them, I'm afraid.

JANE PARSONS I .... That's

certainly something ....

....

Reacts to Yves's reason

Extract 3

YVES GUILLET So, our proposal is to create a completely new name which will reflect the identity and role of the new company.

Makes a proposal

PETER JOHNSON .... a French name, ... ?

Asks for clarification of FCF's proposal

PASCALE LANNOY ....

It could be a name which reflects both our backgrounds.

Corrects and expands

PETER JOHNSON Right. Well, ...

.... our name not being known in

France, and being very English, ... I think there's a danger in creating a completely new name ...

Reacts to FCF's proposal

Extract 4

PETER JOHNSON   Maybe a better solution would be to combine both our names.   *Makes a proposal*
What's your reaction to that?

PASCALE LANNOY   Well ....   *Reacts to Peter's proposal*

.... that would be.

Check your answers in the key   **B1.2**

B2 Interaction summary

At the stage of making and reacting to proposals or bids it is important to clarify your understanding of what the other side is proposing.

- Clarification can focus on the *interests* which the other party wants to fulfil through that proposal, or on the details of their proposal. The other party can then *confirm* your understanding, or *correct* it, and expand on the point (as you saw in Unit 4).

Asking for clarification of interests

So,	**if I understand you correctly** **if I'm not mistaken**	*you feel* *that ... ?*

Confirming and expanding

That's right. **Exactly!**	*What's more ...*

Asking for clarification of details

You mean **Do you mean**	*a French name* *an agency fee*	**then?** **when you say ... ?**

Correcting and expanding

Not necessarily. **That's not quite what I meant.**	*It could be ...*

It is also important at this stage to acknowledge the other party's proposals and reasons by reacting to them.

- The reaction you choose will show how sympathetic or not you feel towards the reasons and proposals.

Reason

The name Clark-Maxwell is familiar to multinational clients.

Sympathetic reaction

I see what you mean.

Reason

The name is not known in France and sounds very English.

Reservations

I appreciate that. **I take your point(s) about ... ,**	*However, ...* *but ...*

Proposal

Maybe a better solution would be to combine both our names.

Sympathetic reaction

That's certainly worth considering.

Reservations

I'm not sure how realistic that would be.

B3 Tasks

1. The dialogue below is part of a later discussion between Clark-Maxwell and FCF about personnel in the new company. Complete the gaps in the dialogue using the most appropriate expressions from the Interaction summary.

Use the notes on the right to help you.

Notes

JANE PARSONS As you know, many of our methods of training are very specific to us, and are a feature of the Clark-Maxwell approach. Therefore we propose that the trainers in the new company should, at least initially, all be from the British company.

Gives reason

Makes a proposal

YVES GUILLET **a.** .... you feel that using our trainers would be less effective?

Asks for clarification of Clark-Maxwell's interests

JANE PARSONS **b.** .... It's not to say that your trainers couldn't do the job eventually, but we'd need to teach them our methods first.

Confirms and expands

PASCALE LANNOY **c.** .... a formal long-term training programme

.... teach them your methods?

Asks for clarification of details of the proposal

JANE PARSONS **d.** .... One way to do this would be for them to accompany our trainers on courses and learn by watching them work.

Corrects and expands

YVES GUILLET **e.** ....

Reacts sympathetically

> Check your answers in the key **B3.1**

2. You are the General Manager in the UK of a chain of Italian men's clothes shops. You are going to take part in the bidding stage of a short negotiation with a representative from the Italian Head Office of the company about a line of men's overcoats. His part of the discussion is on the tape. Study the interaction plan below and prepare what you want to say.

🔲 When you are ready, listen to tape B3.2 and play the role of the British Sales Manager.

The Head Office representative starts

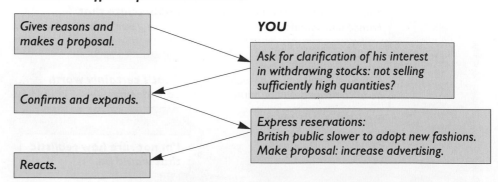

🔲 Now listen to the complete interaction on tape B3.3.

C Style – How to maintain a climate of cooperation

C1 Focus

1. Listen to tape C1. You will hear two extracts from a different version of this stage of the negotiation between Clark-Maxwell and FCF. As you listen, answer the questions below.

    a. How often do the speakers ask for clarification of the other party's interests?

    b. How often do the speakers ask for clarification of the details of the other party's proposals?

    c. How do the speakers react to the other party's reasons and proposals?

Compare your ideas with those in the key **C1.1**

2. Now play tape C1 again and compare the recorded extracts with the original versions written below.

Compare Extract 1 with this:

PARSONS: ... Therefore, we propose that the new company in France should also have the name Clark-Maxwell.

LANNOY: I see. So, if I understand you correctly, you feel that using the name Clark-Maxwell in France too will give the new company a clear identity in the eyes of multinational clients.

JOHNSON: That's right. And what's more, our best-known training package, the Total Quality Management Programme, is associated with our name.

GUILLET: I appreciate that. Of course multinational clients are very important. However, we shouldn't forget that one of our objectives in forming this new company is to enter new markets. We feel that the biggest potential in France for the products and services of the new company is among medium-sized French companies. Many of these companies will never have heard the name Clark-Maxwell. It will mean nothing to them, I'm afraid.

PARSONS: I see what you mean.

Compare Extract 2 with this:

GUILLET: So our proposal is to create a completely new name which will reflect the identity and role of the new company.

JOHNSON: You mean a French name, then?

Now put a tick (✔) in one (or more) of the boxes below.

The versions recorded on tape C1 are:

a. more effective   ☐

b. less effective   ☐   than the original versions above.

c. more confrontational   ☐

Compare your ideas with those in the key **C1.2**

C2 Style summary

In order to maintain the climate of cooperation, there are certain choices about the *style* of language which can be made at the bidding stage.

- Use of clarification, both of interests and details.

  A: *I don't think we could agree*   ⟶   A: **You mean a French name, then?**
  to having a French name.

  B: *We didn't say it had*   ⟶   B: **Not necessarily.**
  to be a French name.

- Use of expressions to show you understand the other side's reasons even if you don't accept them completely.

  I don't agree at all.   ⟶   **I appreciate that.** *Of course*
  Multinationals will not be the   *multinational clients are very important.*
  focus of the new business.   *However, …*

  I'm not sure about that!   ⟶   **I see what you mean.** *That's*
  certainly something we'll have
  to take into account.

C3 Task

Look at the short dialogue below. It comes from the bidding stage of a discussion about filling a key vacancy in the headquarters of an international company. Rewrite the dialogue, incorporating ideas from the style summary in C2, to make the discussion more cooperative.

TOM: I think we should promote Pablo Jimenez. He's creative and he's dynamic.

PAT: I don't agree at all. He's far too young. I propose that we offer the job to Edward Smythe – he's been with us for 15 years now and knows the company very well.

TOM: You can't be serious! This job needs someone with ideas and creativity. Jimenez has got plenty of those.

PAT: That's not how I see it. This is a key position. We need a candidate with experience of the company who's used to making decisions.

Compare your version with the one in the key   `C3`

D Cross-cultural differences – What's the explanation?

D1 Focus

Read the short case study, then answer the question at the end.

Paul Matthews, the Marketing Manager of a British producer of computer games, was hoping to break into the Spanish market. He had already been visited by Javier Ramirez, an Account Executive from a top Spanish advertising agency. Paul Matthews had been impressed by Ramirez's ideas and air of efficiency. Having agreed to use Ramirez's agency, Capo Promociones, he set up a meeting in Madrid the following month at which Javier Ramirez would present firm proposals for a Spanish launch.

When Matthews arrived at Capo Promociones' office, he was met by Javier Ramirez and Elena Espiga, who would be helping to launch the computer games on the Spanish market.

During their presentation, Matthews was surprised to find that various people kept coming into the room to ask questions unrelated to the topic under discussion and Ramirez took several telephone calls. When Ramirez was on the phone, Elena Espiga continued the presentation competently and obviously had plenty of ideas about promotional methods in the Spanish market. However, neither of the Spaniards would commit themselves on the question of an exact launch date or on the schedule of advertising events leading up to the launch.

At the end of the meeting, despite being impressed by Capo Promociones' ideas, Matthews had second thoughts about his decision to place his business with them. These were his thoughts after the meeting:

– It's impolite to allow all these interruptions in a meeting.

– Why won't they commit themselves to a firm launch date?

What underlying cultural differences do Paul Matthews' thoughts illustrate?

Now read the comments in the summary.

D2 Cross-cultural summary

Many people in Mediterranean cultures, such as Spain, have a different attitude to time than those in English-speaking countries and Northern Europe. In a *polychronic* culture, such as Spain, Italy or Greece, there is a high tolerance for many different things happening at once and so meetings may be interrupted by telephone calls and people dropping in with questions.

In contrast, people from a *monochronic* culture such as Britain, Germany or North America, dedicate blocks of time to a certain task or meeting and have a very low tolerance for interruptions and diversions within that block of time.

Differing attitudes to time in *polychronic* and *monochronic* cultures also underlie Paul Matthews' worries about the launch date. In a *monochronic* culture, great emphasis is placed upon deadlines and schedules, and efforts are made to adhere to these. In a *polychronic* culture, attitudes to time are much more flexible, people live much more in the present and, where possible, avoid being tied down to specific dates in the future.

Answer key

A Language

AI.I

a. False b. True c. False d. True

AI 🔲

JOHNSON: Good, that's agreed then. So now we come to the question of the name of the new company. Jane, would you like to give our views on this?

PARSONS: Certainly. As you know, we have an established reputation in the UK, and last year we also set up companies in Germany and Italy. Many of our clients are multinational companies and, in all three countries, they're used to doing business with us under the name Clark-Maxwell. **Therefore, we propose that** the new company in France **should** also have the name Clark-Maxwell.

LANNOY: I see. So, if I understand you correctly, you feel that using the name Clark-Maxwell in France too will give the new company a clear identity in the eyes of multinational clients?

JOHNSON: That's right. And what's more, our best-known training package, the Total Quality Management Programme, is associated with our name.

GUILLET: Oh, I appreciate that. Of course multinational clients are very important. However, we shouldn't forget that one of our objectives in forming this new company is to enter new markets. We feel that the biggest potential in France for the products and services of the new company is among medium-sized French companies. Many of these companies will never have heard the name Clark-Maxwell. It will mean nothing to them, I'm afraid.

PARSONS: I see what you mean. Well, that's certainly something we'll have to take into account.

GUILLET: And there are a couple of other points. **Firstly**, the name Clark-Maxwell sounds very English, and **secondly**, it says nothing about the type of activity the company is involved in. **So our proposal is** to create a completely new name which will reflect the identity and role of the new company.

JOHNSON: You mean a French name, then?

LANNOY: Not necessarily. It could be a name which reflects both our backgrounds.

JOHNSON: Right. Well, I take your points about our name not being known in France, and being very English, but I think there's a danger in creating a completely new name. Existing clients of yours, and ours, might not appreciate the experience and know-how that we've brought to this new venture. It might appear to be a completely new and inexperienced firm. **Maybe a better solution would be to** combine both our names. What's your reaction to that?

LANNOY: Well, I'm not sure how realistic that would be. It would be very long …

AI.2

See tapescript AI above. The missing words are in **bold**.

A3.I 🔲 Model version

a. (Example) The Nigerian subsidiary has been running at a loss for the last two years. Therefore, our proposal is to close it down.

b. Labour costs in Sweden are very high. So, we propose that we should move production to Portugal.

c. The market for personal computers is very competitive. Therefore, our proposal is to concentrate on software development.

d. Developing this new refining process has cost the company a lot of money. Therefore, we propose that we should try to sell it under licence to other companies.

e. Our company is expanding into international markets. So, our proposal is to invest more money in language training.

A3.2 🔲

a. (Example) Maybe a better solution would be to look at ways of making it more cost-effective.

b. Maybe a better solution would be to expand the factory in the UK.

c. Alternatively, we could diversify into other types of office equipment.

d. It could be a good idea to charge a royalty fee too.

e. Alternatively, we could recruit bilingual staff.

B Interaction

B1.1

i. b   ii. b   iii. c

B1 📻

See A1 for tapescript.

B1.2

Extract 1

So, **if I understand you correctly**, you feel …
That's right.
I appreciate that. Oh, of course multinational clients are very important. **However**, we …

Extract 2

I **see what you mean.** That's certainly something **we'll have to take into account.**

Extract 3

You mean a French name, **then**?
Not necessarily.
Right. Well, **I take your points about** our name not being known in France, and being very English, **but**, …

Extract 4

Well, **I'm not sure how realistic** that would be.

B3.1

a. So, if I understand you correctly … *or* So, if I'm not mistaken …
b. That's right   *or*   Exactly.
c. Do you mean … when you say … ?
d. Not necessarily.   *or*   That's not quite what I meant.
e. That's certainly worth considering.

B3.2 📻

REPRESENTATIVE: As you know, this line of men's overcoats has not been very popular since we launched it in Britain last year. So I propose that we withdraw all stocks and return them to Italy.

YOU: ....

REPRESENTATIVE: Exactly. Sales in Italy of these overcoats have been four times higher in the same period.

YOU: ....

REPRESENTATIVE: Well, I'm not sure how realistic that would be.

B3.3 📻 Complete interaction

REPRESENTATIVE: As you know, this line of men's overcoats has not been very popular since we launched it in Britain last year. So I propose that we withdraw all stocks and return them to Italy.

MANAGER: **So, if I'm not mistaken, you feel that we're not selling sufficiently high quantities of these coats?**

REPRESENTATIVE: Exactly. Sales in Italy of these overcoats have four times higher in the same period.

MANAGER: **Well, I take your point about sales,**

but the British public is slower to adopt new fashions. Maybe a better solution would be to increase our advertising for these coats.

REPRESENTATIVE: Well, I'm not sure how realistic that would be.

C Style

C1.1

i.   Not at all.
ii. There is no clarification of proposals.
iii. The reactions are very hostile.

C1 📻

Extract 1

PARSONS: … Therefore we propose that the new company in France should also have the name Clark-Maxwell.

LANNOY: I don't agree at all. Multinationals will not be the main focus of the new business. We feel that the biggest potential in France for the products and services of the new company is among medium-sized French companies. The name Clark-Maxwell will mean nothing to them.

JOHNSON: I'm not sure about that!

Extract 2

GUILLET: … So our proposal is to create a completely new name which will reflect the identity and role of the new company.

JOHNSON: I'm not sure we could agree to having a French name.

LANNOY: We didn't say it had to be a French name.

C1.2

b. and c.

C3 Model version

TOM: I think we should promote Pablo Jimenez. He's creative and he's dynamic.

PAT: So, if I understand you correctly, you feel that creativity and dynamism are important qualities needed in the job?

TOM: Exactly.

PAT: Well, I appreciate that creativity and dynamism are important. However, we mustn't forget that this is a key position. We need a candidate with experience of the company who's used to making decisions.

TOM: Yes, that's a reasonable point. We'll certainly have to consider that aspect, too.

PAT: Edward Smythe has that kind of experience. He's been with us for 15 years and knows the company very well. I propose that we offer him the job.

TOM: Yes, I take your point about his experience, but I don't think he's the right man for this job. Maybe … .

Bargaining

A *Language*	How to link offers and conditions
B *Interaction*	How to react to conditional offers
C *Style*	How to move towards agreement
D *Cross-cultural differences*	What are the different approaches?

Background

A German telecommunications company, Ultratel AG, is considering setting up a production plant in Ireland. They are negotiating with the Irish Industrial Board (IIB) which encourages investment by foreign companies, through a variety of incentives such as tax breaks, capital grants and subsidised training for new employees. Representatives from Ultratel are in Ireland to discuss the details of an incentive package which has been proposed by the IIB.

A Language – How to link offers and conditions

A1 Focus

When both sides have put forward their bids, the negotiation can move into the *bargaining* stage when further *offers* can be made. These offers are frequently linked to certain *conditions*.

🎞 Listen to tape A1. You will now hear part of the discussion between Ultratel and the IIB.

Present at this stage of the negotiation are
Anne Gallagher   IIB
Gunter Schloss   Ultratel
Hans Weber   Ultratel

1. Decide if the following statements are *true* or *false*.
   a. The Germans have suddenly decided that they would prefer to do the training in-company.
   b. The IIB are worried that the German style of training might not be suitable in Ireland.
   c. The Germans refuse to accept a joint training programme.
   d. The IIB's offer of covering some of the training costs is linked to the condition that the Germans agree to a joint training programme.

Check your answers in the key **A1.1**

78 ∎

2. Listen to tape A1 again and complete the missing words in the extract. Then read the notes on the right.

Notes

ANNE GALLAGHER Also, we .... fund an in-company training programme
.... there .... some input from Irish training experts. So, would you be prepared to consider a joint training programme?

Makes an offer linked to a condition

Asks for Ultratel's reaction

GUNTER SCHLOSS Yes, I see what you mean about learning styles. I think, in principle, ... no objection to a joint training programme .... the details .... worked out together. What would the financial implications be?

Accepts the offer, but links it to a condition

Asks a question

ANNE GALLAGHER Well, ... you .... a joint training programme, we .... up to 75 per cent of the costs.

Makes a further offer linked to a condition

Check your answers in the key **A1.2**

A2 Language summary

At the bargaining stage, new offers are usually made in response to the other side's proposals. Both your offers and acceptance of the other side's offers can be linked to conditions.

Linking offers and conditions

Offer	(Link word)	Condition
We **couldn't fund** an in-company training programme,	**unless**	there **was** some input from Irish training experts.
We **could fund** an in-company training programme,	**if**	there **was** some input from Irish training experts.

(Link word)	Condition	Offer
If	you **accepted** a joint training programme,	we **would cover** up to 75 per cent of the costs.

Linking acceptance to conditions

Acceptance	(Link word)	Condition
We'd have no objection to a joint training programme	**provided that**	the details **were** worked out together.

(Link word)	Condition	Acceptance
If	the details **were** worked out together,	we'd be **prepared** to agree to that proposal.

A3 Task

Expand the notes below into offers linked to conditions, or acceptance linked to conditions.

Follow the examples.

a. Example

Link word	if
Condition	you/increase/order to 250 units a month
Offer	we/offer/discount of 2.5 per cent
Model version	**If you increased your order to 250 units a month, we could (*or* would) offer a discount of 2.5 per cent.**

b. Example

Acceptance	we/prepared/accept/offer
Link words	provided that
Condition	discount/come/into effect immediately
Model version	**We'd be prepared to accept your offer provided that the discount came into effect immediately.**

(You can hear these model versions recorded on tape A3.)

c.	Link word	if
	Condition	you/install/equipment yourselves
	Offer	we/drop/total price by 5 per cent
d.	Offer	not/install/equipment ourselves
	Link word	unless
	Condition	you/provide/supervisor
e.	Acceptance	we/prepared/agree/that
	Link words	provided that
	Condition	you/pay/supervisor's expenses
f.	Offer	sign contract immediately
	Link word	if
	Condition	guarantee/single union agreement
g.	Link word	if
	Condition	delays due to subcontractors/excluded
	Acceptance	we/have/no objection to a penalty clause

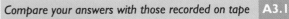

Compare your answers with those recorded on tape **A3.1**

B Interaction – How to react to conditional offers

The German company is only interested in setting up in Ireland if they can find a suitable locally-based supplier of sub-components. The IIB has set up a meeting between Irish Electrical Systems, a potential supplier, and Ultratel. As the Germans are very concerned about quality and engineering standards, one condition they have imposed is that the supplier should buy new production equipment and re-train their workers to Ultratel's specifications.

B1 Focus

At the bargaining stage of the negotiation it is important to respond clearly to the other side's offers.

🔲 Listen to tape B1. You will now hear an extract from the bargaining stage of a negotiation between Ultratel and Irish Electrical Systems. Present at this negotiation are
David Sullivan   Irish Electrical Systems
Hans Weber   Ultratel

1. Answer the following questions.
   a. David Sullivan wants Ultratel to guarantee orders worth £200,000 in the first year.
      Does Hans Weber:
      i. reject this request?
      ii. accept it?
   b. Hans Weber's first offer is £200,000 of orders in the first two years.
      Does David Sullivan:
      i. reject this offer?
      ii. accept it?
   c. David Sullivan requests £275,000 worth of orders over two years. Hans Weber accepts this on a condition.
      Does David Sullivan:
      i. reject this condition?
      ii. accept it?

   | Check your answers in the key | B1.1 |

🔲 2. Listen to tape B1 again and complete the missing words in the extracts. Then read the notes on the right.

Extract 1

		Notes
DAVID SULLIVAN	… We'd only be prepared to spend that kind of money if you guaranteed us orders worth around £200,000 in the first year.	
HANS WEBER	.... guarantee that much in the first year,	*Rejects this offer*
	.... to guarantee minimum orders worth £200,000 in the first two years.	*Makes an alternative offer*
DAVID SULLIVAN	.... that .... make our investment worthwhile.	*Rejects this offer*

Extract 2

HANS WEBER In that case, I'd propose guaranteed orders worth £250,000 over two years. How does that sound to you? *Makes another offer*

DAVID SULLIVAN If you increased that to £275,000, ... *Offers acceptance on a condition*

....

Extract 3

HANS WEBER … our quality control engineers to inspect the new equipment when it's been installed.

DAVID SULLIVAN Yes, I think .... *Accepts unconditionally*
with that.

Check your answers in the key B1.2

B2 Interaction summary

Your responses to the other side's offers can range from rejection through to unconditional acceptance. Particularly when dealing with native speakers of English, it can be important to reduce the force of a rejection by using the introductory phrase *I'm afraid*.

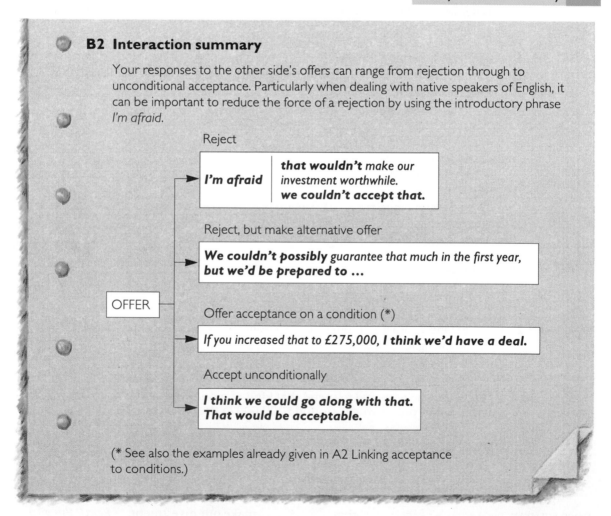

Reject

| **I'm afraid** | **that wouldn't** make our investment worthwhile. **we couldn't accept that.** |

Reject, but make alternative offer

We couldn't possibly guarantee that much in the first year, **but we'd be prepared to …**

OFFER

Offer acceptance on a condition (*)

If you increased that to £275,000, **I think we'd have a deal.**

Accept unconditionally

I think we could go along with that.
That would be acceptable.

(* See also the examples already given in A2 Linking acceptance to conditions.)

B3 Tasks

1. Listen to tape B3.1. First, you will hear someone making an offer linked to a condition. Respond following the written instruction. Then you will hear a model version.

Follow the example.

a. Example

You hear	We'd be prepared to subsidise up to 75 per cent of the training costs.
Instruction	Offer acceptance on a condition: 80 per cent
You	....
Model version	**If you increased that to 80 per cent, I think we'd have a deal.**

b. Instruction	Accept unconditionally.
c. Instruction	Reject.
d. Instruction	Reject, but make alternative offer: 75 per cent reduction in the first year.
e. Instruction	Offer acceptance on a condition: guaranteed minimum of 500 people.

2. You are the owner of a restaurant. You are negotiating with a wholesaler about discounts on the supply of wine to your restaurant.

Listen to tape B3.2 and follow the interaction plan as you play the role of the buyer.

The wholesaler starts

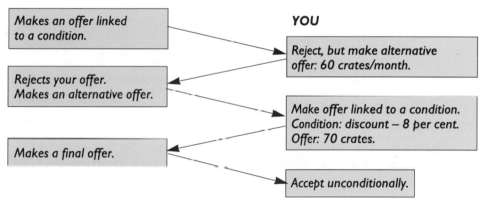

Now listen to the complete interaction on tape B3.3.

C Style– How to move towards agreement

C1 Focus

1. Listen to tape C1 and complete the missing words in the extracts below.

(**Note:** In these extracts you will be focussing on different aspects of the dialogue from those in section B1.2.)

Extract 1

DAVID SULLIVAN I'm afraid that wouldn't make our investment worthwhile.

However, if .... prepared to negotiate on the basis of two years' guaranteed orders, I .... be able to get the Board to agree to the investment.

Extract 2

DAVID SULLIVAN   If you increased that to £275,000, I think we'd have a deal.

HANS WEBER   OK, ... to £275,000 of guaranteed orders

in the first two years provided that you .... our quality control engineers to inspect the new equipment when it's been installed.

Check your answers in the key   **C1.1**

2. Now compare the sentences in the extracts above to this sentence:

We'd only be prepared to spend that kind of money if you guaranteed us orders worth around £200,000 in the first year.

Put a tick (✔) in one of the boxes below.

The sentences in C1.1 show that the speakers are:

a. closer to agreement   ☐

b. further from agreement   ☐   than in C1.2.

Compare your ideas with those in the key   **C1.2**

C2 Style summary

At the bargaining stage of a negotiation, concessions are commonly signalled by a change in the language pattern of the offer/acceptance linked to a condition:

from (where the parties are further apart)	to (where the parties are closer to agreement)
We **would** be prepared to ... if you **guaranteed** us ... →	We**'ll** agree to ... provided that you **allow** ...
We **couldn't** fund ... unless there **was** ... →	We**'ll** be able to deliver ... provided that there **is** ...
If you **were** prepared to ... I **might** be able to ... →	If you **accept** ... I **may** be able to ...

Although offers/acceptances made in the form on the right are still linked to conditions, the offer/acceptance is much firmer and is a signal that the negotiators are *moving towards agreement*. Therefore, this type of offer/acceptance is more commonly made at later phases of the bargaining stage.

C3 Tasks

1. A client of a top quality Hong Kong hotel is negotiating compensation for a mistake in her hotel booking. Match phrases from columns A and B below to form complete sentences which are either offers/acceptances linked to conditions, or firmer offers/acceptances linked to conditions.

Follow the example.

A	B
a. If you're prepared to negotiate on the basis of five visits,	i. what would you be prepared to offer?
b. If I guaranteed you my next five bookings,	ii. provided that you confirmed your booking a month in advance.
c. If you accept a two-week period of notice,	iii. I may be able to increase the discount.
d. We'd offer a 10 per cent discount on every visit,	iv. if you were to offer a more substantial discount.
e. I would consider guaranteeing you my bookings for those trips,	v. I'll guarantee you my bookings for the next five trips at 10 per cent off.

Check your answers in the key C3.1

2. Now use the complete sentences from C3.1 to complete this negotiation. Use the notes on the right to help you.

Notes

CLIENT In view of the fact that I'm a regular client, I'd like to know what kind of compensation you plan to offer me.

MANAGER Well, Mrs Farrant, we apologise for the inconvenience, and we'd be happy to offer you a discount of 5 per cent on your next booking.

CLIENT Actually I had a rather higher figure in mind. My company can get 5 per cent from your main competitor any time. And I'm planning at least five more trips to Hong Kong this year.

.... *Offer linked to condition*

....

MANAGER Well, ... *Firmer offer linked to condition*

....

CLIENT I see. So .... *Asks for his offer linked to condition*

....

MANAGER .... *Offer linked to condition*

....

CLIENT I'm afraid I couldn't always plan that far in advance.

However, ... *Firmer acceptance linked to condition*

....

MANAGER I think we could go along with that.

Check your answers in the key C3.2

D Cross-cultural differences – What are the different approaches?

D1 Focus

1. Different cultures approach meetings and negotiations in different ways. The chart below compares three main cultural groups – Japanese, North Americans and Latin Americans – in terms of five key areas. Some of the information is missing and can be found below the chart. Put the information in what you believe to be the correct box.

   Follow the example.

	Japanese	North American	Latin American
Emotions	Emotions are valued but must be hidden.	1. *C*	2.
Power	3.	Power games are played all the time. To be strong is highly valued.	4.
Decision making	5.	6.	Decisions are made by individuals in charge.
Social interaction	7.	Face-saving does not openly matter. Choices are usually made on a cost/benefit basis.	8.
Persuasion	Not very argumentative. Quiet, patient and respectful. Modesty and self-control are highly valued.	9.	10.

a. Emphasis is on reaching agreement and consensus.
b. Face-saving is extremely important. Choices are often made on the basis of saving someone from embarrassment.
c. Emotions are not highly valued. Interactions with others are mostly unemotional.
d. Passionate and emotional when arguing. Enjoy a warm interaction as well as a lively debate.
e. Emotional sensitivity is valued. Interactions can be highly emotional and even passionate.
f. Great power plays. To be stronger than the others is particularly valued.
g. Decisions are made by the group rather than individuals.
h. Face-saving for oneself is critical to preserve honour and dignity.
i. Always ready to argue their point of view in an impersonal way. Arguments are based on facts.
j. Team work provides input to decision makers.

Check your answers in the key **D1.1**

2. Now think about your own culture and how you would respond in terms of these five key areas. If you have the opportunity, discuss it with other colleagues.

Now look at the cross-cultural summary below.

D2 Cross-cultural summary

Previous units have looked at many of the underlying assumptions that make cultures different and therefore may lead to communication problems. These assumptions include attitudes to time, the role of silence, relationships between superiors and subordinates, and the emphasis placed on individual or group activity. The combination of many of these attitudes and assumptions influences the way in which people behave in specific situations such as negotiating. For example, the different methods of persuasion, described in the chart for the three cultures, reflect their different attitudes to the importance of group harmony contrasted with individual performance, and to the role and value of silence.

An awareness and knowledge of these different attitudes, assumptions and ways of behaving will help to reduce the risk of misunderstandings, and even conflict, in international negotiations.

Answer key

A Language

AI.I
a. False b. True c. False d. True

AI 📼

SCHLOSS: My colleague, Mr Weber, and I have been discussing the proposal you made yesterday concerning training for new employees. As you know, quality is very important to us and therefore we try to standardise training throughout the company worldwide. So, on consideration, we would prefer to handle the training in-company.

GALLAGHER: Does that mean that your own trainers would run the programmes?

WEBER: Yes. That's what we usually do.

GALLAGHER: I appreciate that some companies prefer to do their own training, but our main concern in that case would be that German trainers might not take into account the different learning styles in this part of the world. Also, we **couldn't** fund an in-company training programme **unless** there **was** some input from Irish training experts. So, would you be prepared to consider a joint training programme?

SCHLOSS: Yes, I see what you mean about learning styles. I think, in principle, **we'd have** no objection to a joint training programme **provided that** the details **were** worked out together. What would the financial implications be?

GALLAGHER: Well, **if** you **accepted** a joint training programme, we **would cover** up to 75 per cent of the costs.

WEBER: Mmm …

AI.2
See tapescript AI above. The missing words are in **bold**.

A3 📼
a. (Example) If you increased your order to 250 units a month, we could offer a discount of 2.5 per cent.

b. (Example) We'd be prepared to accept your offer provided that the discount came into effect immediately.

c. If you installed the equipment yourselves, we'd drop the total price by 5 per cent.

d. We couldn't install the equipment ourselves unless you provided a supervisor.

e. We'd be prepared to agree to that provided that you paid the supervisor's expenses.

f. We'd sign the contract immediately if you guaranteed a single union agreement.

g. If delays due to subcontractors were excluded, we'd have no objection to a penalty clause.

B Interaction

BI.I
a. i b. i c. ii

BI 📼

SULLIVAN: Look at it from our point of view. You're asking us to invest nearly half a million Irish pounds in new production equipment and training in order to meet your specifications. We'd only be prepared to spend that kind of money if you guaranteed us orders worth around £200,000 in the first year.

WEBER: **We couldn't possibly** guarantee that much in the first year, **but we'd be prepared** to guarantee minimum orders worth £200,000 in the first *two* years.

SULLIVAN: **I'm afraid** that **wouldn't** make our investment worthwhile. However, if you're prepared to negotiate on the basis of two years' guaranteed orders, I may be able to get the Board to agree to the investment.

WEBER: In that case, I'd propose guaranteed orders worth £250,000 over two years. How does that sound to you?

SULLIVAN: If you increased that to £275,000, **I think we'd have a deal**.

WEBER: OK, we'll agree to £275,000 of guaranteed orders in the first two years provided that you allow our quality control engineers to inspect the new equipment when it's been installed.

SULLIVAN: Yes, I think **we could go along** with that.

B1.2

See tapescript B1 above. The missing words are in **bold**.

B3.1 📼

a. (Example) Prompt: We'd be prepared to subsidise up to 75 per cent of the training costs.
   You: ....
   Model version: **If you increased that to 80 per cent, I think we'd have a deal.**

b. Prompt: We couldn't install the equipment ourselves unless you provided a supervisor.
   You: ....
   Model version: **I think we could go along with that.**

c. Prompt: We'd sign the contract immediately if you guaranteed a single union agreement.
   You: ....
   Model version: **I'm afraid we couldn't accept that.**

d. Prompt: We'd be looking for a complete tax break for the first year.
   You: ....
   Model version: **We couldn't possibly offer that much, but we would be prepared to offer a 75 per cent reduction in the first year.**

e. Prompt: We'd be hiring a minimum of 500 people in the first 18 months.
   You: ....
   Model version: **Provided that was a guaranteed minimum of 500 people, I think we'd have a deal.**

B3.2 📼

WHOLESALER: Of course, we'd be able to offer you a much bigger discount, if you ordered 80 crates a month.

YOU: ....

WHOLESALER: I'm afraid we wouldn't be able to offer any more than the standard 5 per cent discount for 60 crates. How about 70 crates a month? Could you manage that?

YOU: ....

WHOLESALER: I'm afraid we couldn't offer that much. I'll tell you what. We'll give you a 6 $^1/_2$ per cent discount on that number.

YOU: ....

B3.3 📼 Complete interaction

WHOLESALER: Of course, we'd be able to offer you a much bigger discount if you ordered 80 crates a month.

BUYER: **We couldn't possibly guarantee to buy that number, but we'd be prepared to take 60 crates a month.**

WHOLESALER: I'm afraid we wouldn't be able to offer any more than the standard 5 per cent discount for 60 crates. How about 70 crates a month? Could you manage that?

BUYER: **If you increased the discount to 8 per cent, we'd agree to take 70 crates.**

WHOLESALER: I'm afraid we couldn't offer that much. I'll tell you what. We'll give you a 6 $^1/_2$ per cent discount on that number.

BUYER: **OK, I think we could go along with that.**

C Style

C1 📼

Extract 1

SULLIVAN: I'm afraid that wouldn't make our investment worthwhile. However, if **you're** prepared to negotiate on the basis of two years' guaranteed orders, I **may** be able to get the Board to agree to the investment.

Extract 2

SULLIVAN: If you increased that to £275,000, I think we'd have a deal.

WEBER: OK, **we'll agree** to £275,000 of guaranteed orders in the first two years provided that you **allow** our quality control engineers to inspect the new equipment when it's been installed.

C1.1

See tapescript C1 above. The missing words are in **bold**.

C1.2

a.

C3.1

a. iii   b. i   c. v   d. ii   e. iv

C3.2

CLIENT: In view of the fact that I'm a regular client, I'd like to know what kind of compensation you plan to offer me.

MANAGER: Well, Mrs Farrant, we apologise for the

inconvenience, and we'd be happy to offer you a discount of 5 per cent on your next booking.

CLIENT: Actually I had a rather higher figure in mind. My company can get 5 per cent from your main competitor any time. And I'm planning at least five more trips to Hong Kong this year. **I would consider guaranteeing you my bookings for those trips if you were to offer a more substantial discount.**

MANAGER: Well, **if you're prepared to negotiate on the basis of five visits, I may be able to increase the discount.**

CLIENT: I see. So **if I guaranteed you my next five bookings, what would you be prepared to offer?**

MANAGER: **We'd offer a 10 per cent discount on every visit provided that you confirmed your booking a month in advance.**

CLIENT: I'm afraid I couldn't always plan that far in advance. However, **if you accept a two-week period of notice, I'll guarantee you my bookings for the next five trips at 10 per cent off.**

MANAGER: I think we could go along with that.

D Cross-cultural differences

DI.I

1. c 2. e 3. a 4. f 5. g 6. j 7. b 8. h
9. i 10. d

Settling and concluding

A	Language	How to close the negotiation
B	Cross-cultural differences	What would you do?

Background

This is a continuation of the scenario in Unit 7. Ultratel AG and the IIB are reaching the end of their negotiation about setting up a production plant in Ireland.

A Language – How to close the negotiation

A1 Focus

At the end of a negotiation the participants usually summarise what has been said.

Listen to tape A1. You will now hear the closing stage of this negotiation between Ultratel and the IIB.

Present at this stage of the negotiation are
Anne Gallagher   IIB
Gunter Schloss   Ultratel
Hans Weber   Ultratel

1. Decide if the following statements are *true* or *false*.
   a. Ultratel have not yet reached a final decision on the location or size of the new plant.
   b. The amount of the capital grant from the IIB for the purchase of a factory has already been decided.
   c. The IIB will be responsible for providing the infrastructure for the factory.
   d. The IIB has now made a final decision on the amount of the grant for training.
   e. There are three main areas for discussion at the next meeting between Ultratel and the IIB.

Check your answers in the key **A1.1**

■ 91

2. Listen to tape A1 again and complete the missing words in the extracts. Then read the notes on the right.

Extract 1

		Notes
ANNE GALLAGHER	Perhaps I could just .... so far.	*Introduces the fact that she wants to summarise*
	.... purchase a factory building of 3,000 m² in the freeport area, and to employ 500 people in this factory, starting in October of next year.	*Summarises the agreements made by Ultratel AG*
GUNTER SCHLOSS	That's correct, yes.	
ANNE GALLAGHER	Fine. And .... , ... give you a capital grant of 45 per cent towards the purchase of the factory.	*Summarises the agreements made by the IIB*
	.... of the infrastructure, and ...	*Recaps on the IIB's agreed responsibility*

Extract 2

ANNE GALLAGHER	Good. So there are a couple of	*Introduces the areas which have not yet been agreed upon*
	.... the Irish contribution to the training programme	*Identifies the first area*
	In order to do this, ... a meeting for you with representatives of the government training authority, so that .... our next meeting, ... worked out the joint programme ...	*Identifies an action point* *Identifies an action point to be completed before the next meeting*

Extract 3

ANNE GALLAGHER	Fine. So, ... the questions of training, recruitment, and also the trade union, in greater detail .... our next meeting, ... the third of February.	*Summarises the points to be discussed and the date for the the next meeting*
	.... everything?	*Checks that nothing has been left out*

Check your answers in the key   **A1.2**

A2 Language summary

- At this stage of the negotiation it is important to *summarise* what *agreements* have already been reached and what responsibilities have already been assigned.

Introducing the summary

Perhaps I could just summarise our	conclusions agreements decisions	**so far.**

Summarising agreements and responsibilities

You've We've	**agreed to ...**	

As we agreed,	**we'll you'll**	take care of ... be responsible for ... deal with ...

- It is also important to identify any areas which have not yet been agreed on and any further *action* which needs to be taken. Finally, any points to be dealt with at the next meeting should be summarised, and a date fixed. It is also helpful to check that there is nothing else which the other side wishes to add.

Identifying the areas which have not yet been agreed on

There are	a couple of some	**outstanding points.**

The question of ... remains to be clarified.

Identifying action to be taken

We'll You'll	set up a meeting ... get further information about ...

By our next meeting **you'll have**	worked out the joint programme ... modified the technical drawings ...

Summarising points and setting a date for the next meeting

We'll discuss the questions of ... **at** our next meeting **on** ...

Checking

Have I covered everything?
Is there anything else you'd like to add?

A3 Task

Below you will see some notes which David Sullivan of Irish Electrical Systems made at the end of his negotiation with Hans Weber. Use these notes to help you with this task of closing the negotiation. You represent Irish Electrical Systems.

ORDERS
- Ultratel guarantee £275,000 in first two years

PRODUCTION EQUIPMENT
- We agree to invest up to £450,000

Action:
- > Ultratel to supply us with technical
  specifications (mid-February)

TRAINING
- We agree to invest up to £15,000

PRODUCTION SCHEDULES   **NEXT MEETING:** 15 March
- > Next meeting   - Production schedules

Listen to tape A3. You will hear eight instructions. After each instruction there is a pause for you to respond. You will then hear a model version.

Follow the example.

Example

Instruction 1	Introduce the summary.
You	....
Model version	**Perhaps I could just summarise our conclusions so far.**

B Cross-cultural differences – What would do you do?

Check some of your cultural assumptions here.

Put a tick (✓) in the *Yes* or *No* column in each case.

	Yes	No
a. I always try to get a written record of what has taken place at significant stages of the negotiation.		
b. I like to have at least one legal expert in my negotiating team who is present for most of the negotiation.		
c. The conclusion of a negotiation is an appropriate time to give a gift to the other side.		

Now read the cross-cultural summary on page 95 for a comment on each assumption.